A Passage
to Peshawar

*A British Officer's experiences in
the Indian Army 1944-46*

W. H. PRECEY

Woodfield

First edition, published in 2002 by

WOODFIELD PUBLISHING
Woodfield House, Babsham Lane, Bognor Regis
West Sussex PO21 5EL, England.

© William Precey, 2002

ISBN 1-903953-28-6

Contents

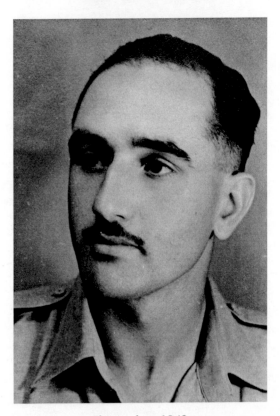

The Author, 1942.

I: Southern Command HQ

My first posting, after a General Staff course at Bulford in the county of Wiltshire, was to Southern Command Headquarters at Wilton House. Wilton, although only a small village, is well known internationally for the fine carpets it produces. It is about three miles from the cathedral town of Salisbury.

At the time of my arrival, the war had been under way for some months – it was now early summer in 1940 – and General Montgomery was the General Officer Commanding. Typically, he required every soldier of the rank of major and below, to assemble each Wednesday afternoon at the gates of Wilton House to run around the wall surrounding the house and grounds, about three miles.

At the time, the world mile record holder, Sydney Wooderson, a member of the Pioneer Corps, was available to lead the motley array of soldiers, he finishing in about fourteen minutes, the majority taking half an hour or more.

I used to look forward to the weekly event, as I was a trained athlete, but several of the chaps appeared very distressed at the end of the run, including some of the officers.

Monty also obliged everybody to attend church service on Sunday, unless they were engaged in essential work. Failure to do so meant extra duties.

Not long after my arrival, the duties of GOC were taken over by General Auckinlek, known as 'the Auk'. He was a massive man, very genial and extremely popular, rather more so than Monty, who, it would seem, appeared to come into his own on active service.

Since General Aukinlek had occasion to stay on at Wilton House overnight, for operational reasons, although he had a large house allotted to him only a mile away, there had been installed, in one of the many bathrooms, a king-size bath to accommodate his bulk. I was billeted at a tiny cottage in Wilton village, with rather primitive washing facilities, so when I was on night duty at the headquarters – this came around about once a month – I used to take along a towel and soap and wallow in the luxury of the general's bath. I am also of rather large proportions.

On one occasion I was caught by the senior officer on duty and was extremely lucky to get away with it. I think that the officer must have had a sense of humour and was impressed when I stood up naked in the bath and saluted! Lord Fortescue was the peacetime occupant of Wilton House; he was a nice, pleasant man and held the rank of colonel. He was of course, the lord of the manor and when walking in the village, as he frequently did, the locals would doff their hats in the traditional way.

He was in command of the Home Guard for the whole Command, which covered a large portion of the south of England.

Colonel Fortescue would frequently visit the Home Guard units to watch their drilling and manoeuvres. Some of the men had rifles, but the majority had to make do with broomsticks, as there was a scarcity of weapons after Dunkirk. They would not have been very effective against the German parachutists who were expected, but this did not dampen their enthusiasm.

I had been delegated to assist the colonel in his duties and I sometimes accompanied him on these inspections.

Early in August, some two months after the miracle of Dunkirk, when the might of the German army was poised just twenty miles across the Channel, presumably preparing to invade, I was summoned to the presence of Lord Fortescue. He said that as it was a fine afternoon he had decided to go grouse shooting in the grounds of the house, although it was early in the season and would I arrange for a party from the Pioneer Corps to act as beaters.

I recalled the story about Sir Francis Drake playing bowls at Plymouth while awaiting the arrival of the Spanish Armada.

It was late in the evening of the same day, a Saturday; I was doing my monthly stint of night duty and quite by chance his lordship was the senior duty officer. I had reported to him and had been told that he was not to be disturbed unless some important matter arose. He, of course, occupied one of the most prestigious of the many bedrooms.

They were reached by a wide, sweeping, thickly carpeted stairway, large oil paintings of the colonel's ancestors lining the walls.

3

I descended to my small room on the ground floor, took off my boots and lay down on the bunk bed to read the evening newspaper.

Just after Dunkirk, when the British Army was in something of a shambles, in order to rekindle their morale and to keep them occupied, a large-scale exercise had been mounted, which covered the whole of the Command. This entailed extensive troop manoeuvres and a great deal of organisation, while at the same time the necessary alertness was maintained to monitor any signs of activity by the enemy across the Channel.

My perusal of the newspaper was frequently interrupted by the arrival of a despatch rider, with a teleprinter message giving details of the progress of the exercise. I would give this a cursory glance to see if there was anything of sufficient importance to justify disturbing his lordship and then drop it on the floor with the intention of picking them all up later to collate them.

Again there was a knock on the door and a DR entered and handed me yet another telex. I read it and dropped it to the floor with the others, only to get up and read it again. It began: 'Oliver Cromwell' – *this was the codeword for the invasion.* 'Enemy barges approaching the Isle of Wight. All informed. Copies to 5th Corps, 8th Corps, C in C Western Approaches, C in C Portsmouth.'

I ran up the stairs with the message and knocked on the colonel's door.

"What is it?" he called out, clearly annoyed at being disturbed.

"I have a message, sir, which I think you should see," I replied, after which I opened the door, walked in and handed him the telex. Some of his usual aplomb left him as he read it.

"Well don't just stand there… you know what to do!"

The drill had, of course, been laid on for such an event. I turned and ran downstairs.

My first action was to telephone the general's house and then to send despatch riders into Salisbury to round up the staff, most of whom were billeted in the town. Messages were flashed on the cinema screens, ordering the staff to report back immediately to Headquarters.

In the space of half-an-hour, the place was seething with people, all going about their pre-determined tasks.

It proved to be a probing exercise by the Germans to test our coastal defences and was dealt with very effectively by the RAF, who attacked the barges. Any which survived the attack were soon engulfed in flames from the ignited mixture of oil and petrol which had been pumped through pipes from the beach, out to sea and then ignited.

Little publicity was given to the attempted landing, since it was considered that the damage to German morale would have been greater if there had been complete silence and the barges had just disappeared.

There was a rumour that Colonel Fortescue had been reprimanded by Brigadier Ritchie the General Staff operations chief, as he had alerted the Home Guard without consultation, although it was known that German spies were active in the area and would no doubt have been alerted to monitor the outcome of the probe and report back to Berlin.

Apart from assisting his lordship from time to time, it was my responsibility to up-date the 'Blue Book' which gave the location of all the units in the Command.

This book, together with other important documents, was kept locked up at night in a steel trunk, both for security reasons and as protection in the event of fire. The trunk could be readily transported to a duplicate headquarters located about half a mile away. It was entirely underground and the only clue to its existence was a small clump of trees on a hillside which appeared to be guarded by an armed sentry.

When approaching the copse, one could discern a steel door let into the ground at an angle, a few steps leading down to it. Inside there was a network of rooms, allocated to the various functions of the Headquarters.

We frequently held a drill to evacuate Wilton House and it took only about ten minutes to transfer to the underground hideout. A fleet of cars and trucks was constantly available to transport the staff and essential documents.

In a very short time, we would be established in the hideout and telephones were buzzing. The object of the duplicate HQ was, of course, to enable the headquarters to remain operational in the event of bombing or bombardments.

I had my first glimpse of the Combined Operations room. It was known as 'the cube room', since its height, width and breadth were the same. It was very large, the walls and ceiling covered with ornate decorations and frescos; a very impressive room.

On a table of extremely large proportions was a gigantic relief map of the south of England. Steps on either side led up to a platform overlooking the table on which officers of the three services stood to review the deployment of the Army units, defence of the airfields, deployment of Naval personnel and defence strategy in general.

Although it was commonly accepted that we could expect an attempted invasion before long and that we were poorly equipped to beat off the attack, nobody ever became despondent. In fact there was an air of excitement about the place, as if we were about to experience a most exciting occasion.

Much time had been given to the matter of beach defences. Officers would frequently visit the beaches to try out various contraptions of steel, concrete and dannert wire, with the cooperation of commando forces.

In reality, the main lines of defence were located some way inland, at places specially chosen for strategic reasons; also, there were underground refuges where people could hide to harass the enemy in the event that their town or village was captured.

There were several members of the other services stationed at Wilton House, for combined operational purposes. I was friendly with one of the RAF men, a corporal, who had the task of liaising with Army Intelligence.

Charlie took his job very seriously. Every evening he would make a round of the pubs in Wilton, of which there are several, on a bicycle he borrowed from the Pioneer Corps. He would have a drink at each pub before cycling on to the next. His capacity was phenomenal. I never knew him to show any signs of being drunk, except for a glassy look in his eyes.

He used to tell me of some of his experiences in Intelligence. A lot of information was obtained from prostitutes who frequented the pubs. They were not local girls. Most of them had come down from London to escape the bombing.

On one occasion, he was told of a secret anti-aircraft battery which was to be installed on Southsea Common, near Portsmouth, on the seafront, to attack German bombers.

Some months later, 'Z' batteries were located on the common. These batteries comprised 64 medium-calibre guns, whose direction and firing were centrally controlled. Initially they were aimed at the enemy wherever they were spotted, but the descending deluge of shell cases did so much damage to buildings in Southsea town they were latterly fired only seawards.

Since the shells exploded almost simultaneously, the effect on the German raiders was devastating. A hit could be made with a deviation of 1,000 feet.

The girl who had told Charlie of the Z batteries, long before they were installed, had learned about them from an intoxicated RAF officer.

However, Charlie's most remarkable story, which I found very hard to believe, but which was confirmed in a report I heard

8

about later, concerned a staff car arriving at Old Sarum fighter base, near Salisbury, driven by an RAF corporal; the passenger was a very senior Air Force officer. This car was accompanied by another, with a wing commander and a group captain as passengers.

The party alighted at the orderly office and the deputy station commander was called – the commander was absent at a conference – and was told they had come from Fighter Command to carry out an inspection.

The officer gave them a full tour of the station. They inspected the installations and the Spitfires and Hurricanes in their hangars, asking many searching questions.

Later, when the station commander returned and telephoned Fighter Command to enquire why he had not been informed of the visit, he was told that they knew nothing about it.

No trace was ever found of the impostors.

We were allowed one day a month from our duties; we worked every day of the week and much of this day off was spent in the Forces canteen in Salisbury.

On one occasion I went into the canteen toilet for a wash, took off my rather valuable watch – a birthday present – and placed it together with my hat – blue with a distinctive headquarters badge – on the shelf above. I bent over to wash my face and straightened up to find that both watch and hat had disappeared, with no sign of the thief.

The military policeman who apprehended me on my walk back to Wilton, hatless, was rather nonplussed when I asked him where I could get another hat on a Sunday evening, having explained, the reason for my bareheadedness.

My home at that time was near London, about fifteen miles south, in Kent, where I lived with my mother. Occasionally I would take a chance on my day off and catch a train from Salisbury to Waterloo Station in London and then a local train to my home station.

I ran the risk of being arrested when I arrived at Waterloo without a pass, but somehow I always managed to dodge the military policemen, who were conspicuous with their red hatbands.

The nearest I came to being caught was on one occasion when I was leaning out of the carriage window, awaiting the departure of the train for Salisbury, when a military police warrant officer who knew me quite well, passed by. I froze. He was on permanent security duty at Headquarters because of his disability. He had a glass eye. Luckily, I was on his blind side when he passed.

When the train arrived at Salisbury, I had to hold back and wait for the next bus to Wilton.

On one other occasion, when I did have a pass and travelled to London on leave, I arrived just after a massive bombing raid had ended. There were no local trains running and everything was in darkness. I set off to walk the fifteen miles or so to my home.

Fortunately, it was a fine night and I had the moonlight to assist me on my journey. The devastation was frightening.

I went past a railway station in south London on which a land mine had been dropped. The station had almost disappeared and there was a colossal hole in its place. A train a little way up the line had all its coaches still ablaze. Firefighters were tackling the conflagration. I was told that there was no way I could help as there were no survivors.

I had not walked very far, still in the south of London. I seemed to have lost my way. I came across another horrific scene. A bus had plunged down an enormous hole which I heard later had been caused by a bomb going down a ventilation shaft adjacent to an Underground railway station. Hundreds of people had taken shelter on the station platforms and the station had collapsed on top of them.

I continued my homeward walk, having somehow found the right direction. Leaving London behind I found myself walking down narrow, unlit country lanes with no sound except for the occasional night owl or a church clock in the distance ringing out the time. I checked with my watch. Twelve fifteen … twelve thirty … one o'clock.

Eventually, after what seemed ages, I arrived home, much to the relief of my mother. Our village was away from the bombing, but there was an RAF fighter station not far away and my mother knew from their level of activity that London must be undergoing another severe attack and that I would be travelling via Waterloo.

Not far from our house was a swimming pool, a rather primitive affair. The water was not very deep. Surrounding the diving board was a fence made of steel piping. Rather foolishly, I suppose, I used to dive off the fence, flattening out on entering the water, so as not to hit the bottom.

I visited the pool during this home leave, even though it was rather early in the year. As I dived off the fence, my feet slipped and I fell headlong into the pool, hitting my head on the bottom. It was a miracle I did not break my neck. I was semi-conscious as some onlookers dragged me out of the pool. I had bitten my tongue and blood was streaming out of my mouth.

For some time after the accident, I suffered periodic black-outs. I could probably have obtained a discharge from the Army. I did get a number of sick leaves. Eventually the Army medical officer at headquarters decided to recommend me for a posting because of the long hours and pressure of work. I was transferred to a supply depot in Portsmouth, right in the middle of the intensive bombing of that city, the premier naval port in the United Kingdom.

It was going to do nothing for my headaches…

II: Portsmouth and the Blitz

It may seem surprising that the Command Headquarters had not been bombed by the Germans, as they undoubtedly knew its location, since Portsmouth, only 60 miles away, had been subjected to repeated attacks from 11th July 1940.

It was reasoned that the enemy considered destroying the headquarters would not be much of an achievement until an invasion was imminent.

A massive attack was made on Portsmouth on the afternoon of Saturday 12th August, when the streets were crowded with shoppers. More than 60 bombs were dropped and 117 people were killed. There was a direct hit on the Princes Theatre.

The raids for the rest of the year were lighter, but the worst was yet to come. On the night of January 10th 1941, 300 German bombers made a concentrated attack on Portsmouth, showering the city with high explosives and incendiaries. The fire blitz had begun.

One of the first bombs to fall, destroyed the electricity generating station, plunging homes, defence centres and shelters into darkness. An added hazard was a stream of blazing alcohol which ran down the road towards the generating station after a nearby bonding store caught fire.

Throughout Portsmouth, candles and oil lamps had to be used, their light insignificant compared to the glare of the scores of fires started by incendiary bombs.

Buildings tumbled and burned, with no hope of the fire fighting services dealing with them. Three main shopping centres and several hotels were reduced to ruins, and among other buildings destroyed were six churches, three cinemas, a school, one hospital and part of the major Royal Hospital.

The Royal was the hospital I attended when I arrived in Portsmouth to take up my duties a few days earlier. I had been told to report there on arrival to have x-rays taken following my diving accident, since it was a large hospital with all the latest modern facilities. In fact, it was going to take them three days to develop the x-rays.

When I returned to the hospital after the bombing I found great difficulty in locating the wing which had housed the x-ray and other technical departments.

I asked a passer-by if he knew where the building was, he merely pointed to a massive hole filled with rubble. No doubt my x-ray was among the debris. Not surprisingly, I never did know the result of the examination; but now there were far more important matters to concern me.

The casualties after the January 10th bombing were, perhaps, light, in view of the scale of the attack. 171 people were killed and 430 injured. Had it not been for the very effective shelters, the casualties would have been much greater. Three thousand people, however, were left homeless.

The night had been horrific, in the true sense of the word. Coming off duty, I had decided to go to the Odeon cinema in town, which, surprisingly was still showing movies. It had been closed but the decision to reopen it had been made in response to public demand, since the bombing had made any other form of entertainment impossible.

The cinema was some way from the barracks; I travelled alone as I had not had time to make any friends. The barracks in which I was billeted were near the naval dockyard. I caught a bus.

Not long after the performance started, we could hear the wailing of sirens warning of the approach of enemy bombers and shortly afterwards we heard the familiar sound of exploding bombs.

Parts of the ceiling started to fall in and the evacuation of the cinema began. The audience did not panic. By this time the residents of Portsmouth had become hardened and well disciplined. Some casualties were carried out.

I arrived in the street to find the night sky illuminated with a rosy glow. There were no buses running and rather than go into a shelter I decided to walk back to the Barracks. I was due on duty a few hours later, fire fighting, and did not wish to let my colleagues down.

At the end of the road, I saw what I thought to be a parachutist about to land, but it was a land mine. The German land mines floated down on parachutes and exploded with devastating effect when they landed, scything down buildings and anything that was standing.

Although I was some way from the blast, I was blown off my feet. I took another turning and eventually arrived at the barracks after a nightmare journey of chaos and destruction. They had taken a severe hammering from the bombers. There was little sign of life.

I heard the distant sound of a radio. It must have been left on when the occupants fled to the shelters, but no other sound.

When I reached what was left of my block, I saw some chaps feverishly digging around an Anderson shelter, which was still intact but was in a large pool of water. I joined in the digging and eventually we recovered the bodies of three soldiers.

Tragically, the shelter had not been hit but a bomb landing nearby had burst the water main and they had been drowned.

We removed the bodies to the nearest building we could find that was more-or-less intact. The door and all the windows had been blown out. There was no light. Someone found a candle and we laid out the bodies by its light.

These were old-fashioned barracks with fireplaces. The bomb blast had blown soot down the chimney and everything was covered, with it. The stench of soot was to stay in my nostrils for some time to come.

Incendiary bombs started to fall through the roof of a nearby storage building. At the same time, a line of trucks was set ablaze by more incendiaries I remember thinking at the time that it was foolish to have left them assembled together.

I could see outside just a few soldiers taking refuge behind the rubble. They included a sergeant major, who was presumably in charge. He was, however, so terror stricken that he could take no part in our attempt to remove the incendiaries from the building. I felt rather sorry for him.

About six of us crossed over to the building, entered and mounted the stairway. We did this with some trepidation as only a short time earlier we had been warned that anti-personnel bombs were being fixed to the incendiaries, which detonated if they were disturbed.

However, making use of some shovels we had found, we managed to throw most of the bombs through the windows into the street, where they continued to blaze, harmlessly.

We went outside and stood wondering what to do next, looking at each other. Somebody made a joke about applying for leave, which we all thought hilariously funny. It was not really all that amusing, but it helped relieve the tension.

Occasionally the warships in the harbour, which was not far away, would open fire with their large-diameter guns. The noise was like an express train going skywards. This was heartening, but the howling gale from the firing swept around, throwing debris in all directions.

I had not slept for at least three nights and by now I was desperately tired. The atmosphere of doom in the barracks decided me to search elsewhere for a place to rest. The bombing had ceased and the all clear had been sounded.

I came across a small infants school, which I entered; it wasn't difficult as the door had been blown off. There were no windows left either and no light except for the glow of the multitude of fires still engulfing the city.

A strong wind was now blowing and the schoolbooks and papers which bestrewed the floor were being swept one way and then the other. There was no desk large enough to accommodate my tall figure but I found what was probably the teacher's chair and I sat down to try to get some sleep.

I remember discerning coloured cut-outs and pictures drawn by the children adorning the wall. These somehow made the whole thing much more bizarre.

I fell into a fitful slumber and awoke early in the morning; it was still dark. The smell of soot lingered around me and reminded me of the previous night's horrific experiences. I longed for the time when I would be able to have a bath.

I had not eaten for a considerable time and decided to venture forth to see if I could find some food and to make contact with the rest of my company, assuming that any of them had survived the bombing of the barracks.

Climbing through a window, I found that I was facing a barricade – from the wrong side. It was being patrolled by an armed soldier, who looked amazed when he saw me. He told me that there was an unexploded bomb under a wall of the classroom where I had been sleeping and he was there to prevent access to the school.

I heard later that the bomb had exploded a few hours after my departure. The school had been demolished. Strangely, all I thought about was the kids' pictures.

I never did meet up again with my colleagues. When I eventually reported to the emergency Army headquarters I found that I had been listed as missing. I gathered that some of my workmates had been killed and the survivors shipped off to another Army barracks to recuperate.

The true number of Army casualties was never made known for security reasons. There was quite a large contingent in Portsmouth, manning the anti aircraft guns and supplying food and ammunition to those troops and to the men manning the sea forts just off Portsmouth and Southsea.

These forts originated in the First World War and were still proving useful as a first line of defence.

After the January 10th bombing, it was recognised by the Army that the troops were being subjected to relentless physical and perhaps more importantly, mental strain and it was made clear to those of us remaining that an application to be posted to another location would be favourably considered.

After I had departed from the school and before I had reported to the emergency headquarters, feeling absolutely starving, I made for the small restaurant in the High Street I used to frequent, not being over enamoured of army food.

I found that the whole street in which it was located, with the exception of the Post Office, had been demolished. I took a very poor view of this.

Overnight, not only had the electricity supply been cut off, again but also the gas and the water. Food was being rationed and water brought in by tanker from outlying villages.

People were queuing outside the Guildhall for their rations. This very tall building, with its imposing clocktower, had also been gutted by incendiaries; just the shell remained.

It was rumoured at the time that the building had been so well protected outside by barbed wire and other entanglements that the fire crew delegated to protect it had been unable to gain entrance and they had to stand by and watch it become enveloped in flames.

I was told by some anti aircraft men that the Germans used the outline of the Guildhall to guide them to the town, when they would shut off their engines and glide in to drop their bombs; in this way they often got through without warning. It was not uncommon for bombs to start falling before the air raid warnings were sounded.

There were, however, barrage balloons, which helped to keep the bombers to a certain height.

It was estimated that 25,000 incendiary bombs were dropped on the night of 10th January. After that, as darkness fell and the warning sirens sounded their dreadful knell, it became routine for the civilian population of Portsmouth to gather up their most treasured possessions, load them into a pram or handcart and trek out of the city to the surrounding hills at Portsdown, much the same as refugees fleeing the German advances on the Continent.

Such was the situation that there was no attempt by the Army to prevent soldiers who were not on duty doing the same. The view of Portsmouth under attack from Portsdown Hill was something not easily forgotten.

Portsmouth's ordeal was officially recognised when Winston Churchill, accompanied by Harry Hopkins, President Roosevelt's special envoy, came to tour the city; a few days later the King and Queen also paid a visit.

On 9th March 1941, the Germans returned again, in a four-hour raid. The following night there was a longer and heavier raid, when nine bombers were shot down, five of them by the Royal Air Force.

The Sailor's Home, a large hotel and a synagogue were burnt out. Yet again, the electricity supply was cut off. Ninety three people were killed and two hundred and fifty injured. The next night, a further twenty-one were added to the city's growing death toll.

April arrived, with no reprieve from the bombers. They came on the nights of April 8, 11 (Good Friday), 17 and 27, causing more heavy damage throughout the city. Two more hospitals were hit during the last attack.

On 17 April, Hayling Island, near Portsmouth, bore the brunt of the attack, as the area was being used as a decoy, to lure the bombers away from Portsmouth Dockyard. Light was allowed to escape from specially constructed buildings and oil-filled drums were set on fire, to simulate burning buildings.

The Germans were now using a new type of incendiary bomb, which burst about thirty feet above the ground and threw out a shower of blazing magnesium.

The facts and figures I have given have been recorded in the archives of the *Portsmouth Evening News*, which never missed a day's publication throughout the terrible ordeal which the city suffered.

On the night of the fire blitz in January, the process department was deluged with earth and other debris when a high explosive bomb hit the adjoining railway line. But the company had prepared for the worst by installing their own power supply for the presses.

I too joined the masses evacuating Portsmouth as darkness fell and the wailing of the sirens heralded yet another bombing attack. There was not a great deal of the city still standing and unless we were on night duty, fire-fighting, there was little point in staying to be subjected to the bombardment.

When we were on duty at night, we lay on our beds with our uniforms on, a blanket over us, awaiting the sound of the sirens. It was difficult to relax and sleep did not come easily. We had to be ready to take off at a moment's notice to assist the fire fighters.

Since there was no Army accommodation left standing, we were billeted anywhere available. I had been temporarily attached to another unit, involved in the distribution of supplies. We were obliged to change our billets on at least six occasions when bomb damage rendered the buildings we were using uninhabitable.

On one occasion, I was taking a bath in the upstairs of a shop we had taken over when a bomb dropped close by. There had been no air raid warning. The door burst open and I stood up as the water sloshed about me. I was reminded of the time in Wilton when I had been discovered using the general's bath.

It is strange how vulnerable I felt without any clothes on. Not that clothes afford much protection from the effects of a bomb.

The windows of the shop had been blown in some weeks earlier, together with the door, and we had boarded the windows up and made a makeshift door. The shop had not been used for business for some time, it had been a greengrocers and there was a smell of rotten cabbage which we could not get rid of.

We obtained tinned food, milk and cornflakes from an Army canteen. Of course, we had access to some of the Army rations we were distributing.

The four of us lived in a kind of splendid isolation, in what had become a sort of ghost town. The rations we were responsible for allocating were collected from underground storage depots by a fleet of trucks, then delivered to the various units that were still functioning. The drivers were real heroes, who carried out their duties under the most appalling conditions.

The population of Portsmouth at this time was, of course, a great deal smaller than in peacetime. Not only were the able bodied men in one or other of the services, the majority going into the Royal Navy, as was traditional, but also most of the young women, many of whom had joined the Women's Royal Naval Service.

In addition, a number of the women worked in factories, secretly located away from the menace of the bombers, producing war materials.

Not to be forgotten were the brave nurses and female ambulance drivers who stayed behind in war-torn Portsmouth to look after the victims of the bombing and to ferry them to safety.

Soon after the declaration of war in September 1939, plans were being implemented to evacuate the children of Portsmouth to outlying villages and to distant towns, where enemy bombing was considered to be unlikely. Most of these children were temporarily adopted by families, some never to see their real parents again.

The time had come for me to leave Portsmouth. It was now late in the summer and the bombing had eased off. The officer in charge of the supply depot considered that a move to the Isle of Wight would be good for me after my long, traumatic spell in the naval town.

III: The Isle of Wight

I crossed over to the Isle of Wight, from Portsmouth to Ryde, by the ferry which plied every hour or so. This was the main route between the Island and the mainland. The service ceased just before nightfall, so that the ferries could avoid being involved in the German bombing raids. This was, of course, a hardship for the Islanders, especially those with relatives on the mainland.

Arriving at Ryde, I caught a bus to Parkhurst, via Newport, the capital of the Island. Parkhurst was a sombre place; in addition to Albany Barracks, where I was to be stationed, it boasted a prison for long-term offenders, a mental hospital and a mortuary.

Since the barracks proper were fully occupied at that time by Marine Commandos, I was housed with my colleagues in a Nissen hut. These ill-conceived edifices, large, soulless constructions of corrugated iron, with concrete floors, were baking hot in the summer and starkly cold in the winter.

Inside, in the centre, were large, cast-iron stoves, which were fed with wood and coal. The smoke escaped through a large-diameter pipe, which went through the roof, but on the occasion when the wind blew in the wrong direction, the smoke would come downwards and fill the hut. Bronchitis in the winter months was a way of life.

The *story* may not have been true, but I was told that some of the commando who occupied the barracks were hardened criminals from the local prison, who had been pardoned on condition that they joined the force for the duration of the war.

I had been promoted to the rank of corporal and my job was to issue food to the troops on the Island, which was a complicated affair since the Island was used extensively as a training ground and so army units came and went at frequent intervals, sometimes taking rations with them that should have been returned.

The supplies were kept in stores, closely guarded, as food for civilians at that time was strictly rationed and attempts could have been made to obtain supplies illegally.

There were frequent inspections, to ensure that the Army supplies were not finding their way onto the black market.

I had to make certain that the records tallied exactly with the stores actually on hand. This was not an easy task, as several of the items were in bulk packs, large boxes of tea and sacks of sugar and flour. Because some of the Army units were small the allocation was a problem.

Inevitably, there were surpluses. Several of the men issuing and delivering the supplies had friends with local families and I turned a blind eye to those of them who took small quantities of cheese, butter and the like to these friends to help supplement their tiny rations.

What made it easy for my conscience were the frequent visits to the depot of a senior supply officer from the mainland, who would regularly collect a large joint of meat for himself, with the blessing of the depot commander.

The barracks were strictly guarded by alert sentries at the main entrance, but there was a gate at the rear which anyone in the know could use. This made life easier for those of us who liked to visit Newport and perhaps stay a little late with friends before returning to our miserable dwellings. Our hut was at the rear of the barracks and so it was easy for us to make discreet exits and entrances.

Since we were only a small unit, we did not qualify for a mess hall of our own and we had to be attached to whichever unit was occupying the barracks, at this time the commandos. The mess hall was large and unfriendly; there were large wooden tables and benches to sit on. We had to queue up with our mess tins for the first course – we each had our own cutlery, which we took with us – then queue again to wash the tin once more for the pudding.

The food was badly cooked and most unappetizing, the tables were filthy. At teatime, plates containing pats of butter and portions of jam in small containers, were placed at each table, but it was not unusual to find on arrival, especially if one was late, that all the butter had gone. It was no use complaining.

Not far from the dining hall was located a NAAFI, a kind of shop-cum-restaurant, run by civilians, where one could purchase food and small domestic items or have a snack. Because of the poor messing arrangements, most of us spent much of our pay there, supplementing our diet.

In sharp contrast to the men of the Commando unit, were their officers, who were always dressed very smartly and obviously modelled themselves on Guards officers, who are well known for their impeccable turnout.

The Orderly Officer came around at mealtimes to enquire whether there were any complaints, but the men were very poor at expressing themselves, except in a jocular fashion, which made no impression, indeed, many of them obviously found the conditions to their liking.

On one occasion a man called out, "It tastes like shit!" but when approached by the Orderly Sergeant added, "but cooked beautifully!" This brought forth howls of raucous laughter.

I made no attempt to voice my opinion about the awful food and the filthy conditions in the mess hall, knowing that as an outsider, I would not be listened to. I did, however, endeavour to enlist the help of my commanding officer in trying to get some improvement, but to no avail. He also conducted himself in a superior manner and was friendly with the Commando officers and clearly did not wish to do anything which might upset them.

When it appeared that food was being stolen from the depot by some of my men, I decided that something drastic had to be done. I had caught one of them hiding food under his mattress and when I challenged him he told me that he was unable to eat the mess hall food and having a wife and child to support on his Army pay, could not afford to buy food in the NAAFI.

One evening I sat down and wrote a letter to the Director of Supplies and Transport at the War Office, Lt-General Kerr, telling him of the situation and asking him if he could do something about it. As a lowly corporal I had absolutely no right to address the general directly, of course.

I sent the letter off and waited for repercussions. It was all of two weeks before anything happened. I was told one morning to report immediately to my CO. He instructed me to proceed forthwith to Newport and to report to the Island Commander. He gave no reason but I guessed what it was about.

I duly reported to Supply Headquarters and was immediately marched ceremoniously into the colonel's office and told to stand at ease. The colonel seemed to be a pleasant character. He regarded me for a few moments with what appeared to be guarded amusement and then his face took on a more serious aspect and he asked me what I thought I was doing, writing to the War Office. Before I could reply, he told me that he had received a message from General Kerr's office, informing him that a major from the Catering Corps and two staff sergeant majors would be coming down to inspect the feeding arrangements at the barracks.

I cannot recall exactly what it was I had written in my letter, but clearly it had made an impact.

Then, rather to my surprise, I was dismissed and told to report back to my unit. I had expected to receive some sort of punishment for my behaviour, but possibly there were no Army regulations covering the sort of misdemeanour I had committed and there was nothing with which I could be charged.

It appeared that at this time my commanding officer was unaware of what was going on, since he did not ask to see me when I returned, to the barracks and I decided to keep quiet about the affair. I knew that it was only a matter of time before he would be informed, as undoubtedly he would be instructed to meet the visitors from London.

I did, however, tell the chaps at the depot and swore them to secrecy. They were jubilant.

I had made myself unpopular to a senior warrant officer of the Commandos, a really hard character, which I suppose was a necessary qualification to handle the men under him. I had mistaken him for an officer at a distance and had saluted him. Their uniforms were very similar and both wore a Sam Browne belt. I was severely told off.

There were civilians in our office, which was another Nissen hut, engaged in keeping records. They were a mixed bunch of people, mostly young women and older men, one of the latter being an Irishman, Paddy, who was very fond of whisky and smoked his pipe incessantly.

Paddy liked to show us his First World War wound. A bullet had passed through his wrist while he was aiming his rifle, when in the trenches and it had then entered his bicep and come out the other side. "Four bullet wounds from one shot!" he used to boast. When he had had too much to drink he would often get into a towering rage, particularly with the officer in charge, who frequently found fault with his work. I got on well with him, however.

One day he came into the office when the officer was there, brandishing a revolver and threatening to shoot him. It was only because of my special relationship with him that I was able to disarm him. I did not feel threatened.

He lost his job and was told not to enter the barracks again. I was sorry to see him go as he had done a lot to liven up the office, but I did keep in touch. The last I heard of him, he was working as a barman in Newport; a job to which he would have been well suited.

One day I decided to go to the NAAFI for some refreshment. It was pouring with rain and one of the girls suggested, jokingly, that I should borrow her umbrella. It was a gaudy affair. Half way across the parade ground, which I should not have crossed anyway, I saw ahead of me the same warrant officer I had saluted in error.

As I approached him I could see clearly through the torrential rain that he was far from amused. He told me to report immediately to the guardroom and await his arrival. He charged me with disorderly conduct – this covered a multitude of Army offences, although I doubt whether walking across a parade ground using a ladies umbrella was one of them – and I was confined to barracks for a week.

I wondered what his attitude would have been if he had known that through my efforts his cookhouse was going to be severely disrupted in the very near future.

I never considered myself to be much of a soldier after all, if it had not been for the war I would have still been working in a shipping office in the City of London, but I always took pride in my appearance. I had kept my dress hat from the time I was working at the headquarters, with the smart brass badge, brightly polished.

One day I had just left the barracks, walking towards Newport, when I spotted a company of commandos, on the other side of the road, being marched towards the barracks by a sergeant.

As we neared each other, the sergeant called out "eyes right" and I realised that he had mistaken me for an officer. Always a quick thinker, I returned the salute smartly and proceeded on my way.

Some time later, I had to appear before my commanding officer, who warned me about my 'unbecoming conduct', as he put it. Apparently someone had seen me saluting the commandos and it had reached his ears. He added that he was concerned about my safety if word should get around that I was responsible for the whole of the Commando unit being put on fatigues to scrub out the cookhouse. He had, therefore, decided to get me away from the barracks for a while and was attaching me temporarily to a unit which had come to the island for extensive battle training.

"About time you did some real soldiering," he said.

It was now April, and proved to be one of the wettest on record, unfortunately, as the 5th Durham Light Infantry, the unit to which I was to be attached, were billeted under canvas on the side of a wooded hill not far from Newport.

I duly reported with my equipment to the officer in charge and was shown to my quarters, which proved to be a bunk bed in one of the dozens of tents, each of which housed about twelve men.

The rain poured down incessantly. There was a sea of mud everywhere. Everything was damp, including our blankets. There was a communal washhouse where we had to strip off to wash in tin basins. There was no hot water. Shaving was agony.

The first day there was a route march across the Island. The Durham Light Infantry have a faster rate of marching than the usual Army infantry. Being unused to this and having long legs, I found it very difficult to keep in step and eventually found myself at the rear of the column, loping along, carrying a Bren gun across my shoulder.

About half way across the island, we were supposed to rendez-vous with the food wagon, but it had got lost, so we had to make do with our emergency rations and water. We pressed on and eventually reached the river Medina, just before nightfall. There we had to find shelter under the trees for the night, with just our Army capes for protection from the rain, but before we were dismissed we were told that we had to dig trenches, as the 'enemy' was just across the river. Tools were produced from the trucks accompanying us and we had to proceed to dig with forks and spades, one man holding a torch and other to dig and then change places. Of course, as fast as we dug, the holes filled with rainwater and the sergeant in charge eventually realized we would not be able to shelter in the flooded trenches and called a halt to the proceedings.

Morning came, overcast and miserable, but it had stopped raining. We had to line up with our mess tins for breakfast. The food wagon had caught up with us.

Breakfast consisted of the usual Army food, baked beans, corned beef and hot, steaming mugs of thick tea, generously laced with sugar and Carnation milk.

Afterwards we assembled for boat drill. This was a new experience for me; I hadn't the least idea what to do, but never lacking in enthusiasm, I somehow muddled through and helped to get one of the collapsible canvas boats erected.

Getting it down to the riverbank and into the river was something of an ordeal, but as so often happens in this kind of circumstance, being still wet from the overnight rain, tired and aching, humour showed through and by the time we were afloat we were laughing and joking. We should, of course, have been silent, as the 'enemy' were supposed to be on the opposite bank.

The assault went off quite well and after we had re-grouped and sorted ourselves out, we began the last leg of the march back to the campsite.

I was still carrying the platoon Bren gun, loping along in the rear. My feet were blistered, not being used to long marches in army boots and it was very painful, however I had no choice but to carry on.

The routes took us through Newport and as we neared the town, we were ordered to march to attention. We must have looked a miserable sight, unshaven, unwashed and weary as we wended out way through the town. Fortunately, it was still early and there were not many people about.

Arriving back at the camp we assembled on parade while a roll call was taken and then were dismissed to check in our weapons. Afterwards we thankfully retired to our tents, took off our uniforms and kit and lay down on our bunks for a well-earned rest.

I had just closed by eyes when the orderly sergeant came around and told us that we were to parade again, immediately. Everybody started cursing. Someone had failed to check in a firearm and this was the sergeant major's way of instilling discipline in his men.

After another half hour or so on parade, we were again dismissed and made for the cookhouse, hunger overcoming fatigue.

The sergeant major was a small man, mild-looking but extremely tough. He had spent some years with the Commandos. He was formerly a schoolteacher. He was not very popular, seeming to have a sadistic streak. One dark evening he was waylaid by some of the chaps, who gave him a beating. He was unable to identify his assailants. The military police were called in, but it was never discovered who was responsible.

Early in the morning he could be heard practising words of command at the top of his voice, over at the back of the woods. Blackbirds would scatter in all directions.

The following day we were on an assault course, down Shanklin Chine, from the road down to the beach.

There were heavy ropes to assist us on the way down, barbed wire and thunder flashes to create battle conditions, also mustard gas. We were not issued with respirators.

I eventually arrived on the beach, my battle dress torn and my legs bleeding from contact with the barbed wire. My rifle barrel was full of mud.

Although it was still early April and quite cold, I walked straight into the sea and wallowed in the surf. Then I was sick, from inhaling some of the gas. I saw that most of the other chaps were also vomiting.

We found our way back up to the road and to the vehicles which were to take us back to the camp.

The next day there was another exercise, across the downs and we had to assault the imaginary enemy with our bayonets. It was not until later, after we had arrived back at the camp, that I discovered that I had lost my bayonet. It was one of the smaller kind, which was strapped to the waist. Of course I had to report the loss and I was ordered to go out early the next morning, using the company bicycle, to try to find it. I was not very hopeful.

Rain had been pouring all night and everywhere was sodden. I went in what I thought was the right direction over the downs and, unbelievably, I stumbled on the bayonet. It was by then extremely rusty.

I returned to the camp and walked through the company lines towards my tent, brandishing the bayonet for all to see. Inevitably, I came across the sergeant major, who screamed at me and ordered me to get the bayonet cleaned and to report back to him in half an hour.

I think he must have still been suffering from the effects of the assault, as he sounded somewhat hysterical. I found that the best way to get the bayonet cleaned was to stick it into the earth a number of times.

The SM never seemed to forgive me for this and was from then on obviously on the alert to see if I misbehaved in any way.

Unfortunately, I was soon in trouble again. There was a sneaky lance corporal, an unlovable type, who never appeared to leave the camp and instead would spend his evenings cleaning equipment for the chaps, for a fee. I had a date one evening and being aware that we were due for weapon inspection early the next morning, I asked him to clean my rifle, for which I paid him. Because of the damp weather they soon bore signs of rust and of course, a dirty rifle in the Army is regarded as a mortal sin.

It was dark when I returned from Newport that evening and I was unable to inspect the rifle until the next morning, when it was too late to do anything with. I discovered that the lance-corporal had not touched it. On parade, the sergeant major, with a gleam in his eye, told me to report immediately to the company office, where I was paraded before the company commander to be severely reprimanded.

The officer said that he would report me to my commanding officer, but never did. He was posted to another unit a few days later and had either forgotten, or more likely, had too much else to concern him.

One evening, when I was in Newport, I met a chap from my depot, who had a couple of ATS girls with him and we celebrated our chance meeting in one of the pubs, staying there with the girls until closing time.

He filled me in with news from the barracks. It was now common knowledge that I was responsible for the cookhouse being turned inside out and although my chaps were rejoicing, the commandos obviously had not taken kindly to being used as skivvies. I viewed my imminent return to the barracks with some misgiving. I am not a physical coward, but the thought of facing irate commandos in large numbers was rather disturbing.

It was extremely dark and very late when I got back to the campsite, feeling rather the worse for drink. Knowing that there were armed sentries about, I crawled in the direction of my tent, through the undergrowth and eventually arrived outside it. Each tent had a large number and I could just discern number 56, which was mine.

I opened the flap and stepped inside with my muddy boots, right on to the face of one of the chaps who had fallen out of bed onto the canvas floor without waking. He was probably drunk also. It did nothing for my popularity.

My month of soldiering finally came to an end and I bade farewell, rather thankfully, to the Durham Light Infantry. It had been another lesson in survival.

Back at the barracks, I learned that we had been allocated rooms in one of the blocks and would be vacating the Nissen hut. The rooms in the barracks were large, Victorian-type, with enormous windows; everything was painted dark brown or dark green; not very attractive, but a great improvement on the hut.

I had been told to report to the office the following morning at ten o'clock, before taking up my duties again and because of this I decided to stay in bed until nine, although I knew that I would miss breakfast, but I felt like a long rest after my month under canvas.

I had forgotten that they sometimes turned off the water about nine in the morning, although I never knew why, with all the rain we had been getting. There couldn't have been a water shortage.

I was lathering my face as the water dribbled to a halt. The mirror was on the wall, near the washroom window and just at that moment a plane dived between the barrack buildings and machine gunned the troops, who were assembled on the parade ground prior to breaking off for their breakfast.

It was a German Stuka, I heard later and there were quite a number of casualties, including one chap killed and three injured from my depot.

I had heard that there was some evidence of spying activity on the Island, when I was at the Headquarters and I was quite convinced that the Luftwaffe would have been told of the assembly each morning at nine on the parade ground. It seemed too much of a coincidence that the attack should have taken place just when the troops were assembled, for quite a short period.

The food in the mess hall had improved dramatically. It was very difficult to appreciate that it was produced from the same rations, issued by our depot, as the muck we had been served before the gentlemen came down from London. We no longer had to scramble for the butter at teatime and there were tables and chairs.

I had come across the major from the Catering Corps, who had stayed on for a while to ensure that things did not deteriorate again. He called in at the supply depot to carry out an inspection. He did not mention my involvement in the affair of the cookhouse and I thought it wise to stay silent also. Very likely he was unaware that it was me who had alerted the War Office to the sad state of affairs.

By a strange coincidence I was to meet this major again, under entirely different circumstances, in India. It was then I discovered that before the war he was a senior chef at the Trocadero Restaurant in London.

I tried to keep a low profile around the barracks, which wasn't easy as I had to be present when rations were issued to the Commando catering staff. They had come under particularly severe criticism for their poor performance.

I was summoned to see my commanding officer, who told me that he had heard my name mentioned in the officer's mess and the commando officers were not very happy with me. He seemed to like me, although I admit that I had been a bit of a burden to him. He told me that a vacancy had occurred for a senior supply man at the main supply depot in Ryde and that he had recommended me for the position.

A few days later I was on my way again. The previous night we held a farewell party in the Rose and Crown pub. It was Saturday and we didn't have to get up early the next morning. We returned to the barracks late in the evening, round the back way as usual, arm in arm, feeling very jolly. I quickly turned in.

I slept in the lower part of a two-tier bunk. The weather had turned very warm – it was by now early summer-and even at night we had the windows wide open, for which I was thankful as so many of the men smoked incessantly. Several of them also played card, almost without stopping when they were not on duty, sometimes all night.

Malcolm, who had the bunk over me, came in some time later. He always took his drinking very seriously, much as Charlie did at Command Headquarters. He climbed laboriously up into his bunk. I dozed off to sleep. The next moment, it seemed, Malcolm came through the door again.

I thought that I was dreaming. He had got out of the bunk for a pee, but the wrong side and had gone through the window, on to the concrete some twenty feet below. We were on the first floor. Apart from a swollen ankle the next morning, he had not sustained any injury.

My new post at Ryde qualified me for the rank of sergeant. The accommodation was much superior and I had my own room to do in as I pleased, no longer being subject to kit inspections, so I could leave the place as untidy as I wished.

I took morning parades to inspect the men, ensuring that their hands were clean, as they were handling food and then reported to the major for the day's instructions.

I had arranged to meet one of the ATS girls in Newport, on the first Saturday night after my move to Ryde. There was an hourly bus service between Ryde and Newport and she was waiting for me under the clock tower in Newport.

We spent a very pleasant evening together, having a meal at one of the restaurants and then going for a stroll. It was warm and we were enjoying each other's company, oblivious of the time, until I suddenly realized that the last bus back to Ryde had left.

It was about twelve miles back to the depot, Susan could not offer to put me up, as they didn't allow men in their quarters and as there were no taxis operating, I decided to walk the three miles to the Parkhurst barracks. When I arrived, I went around the back, as I used to do and managed to gain entrance.

The walk from Newport had been in darkness, as no street – lights were allowed but being in familiar surroundings I was able to find my way about.

I slept in an armchair in the recreation room and slipped out very early the next morning before anybody was about and walked back to Newport to catch the first bus to Ryde.

I arrived back at the depot in time to have a quick wash and a shave before taking the morning parade.

I saw Susan a few more times, making sure that I did not miss the last bus again. She was a hairdresser in civilian life and worked in a salon not far from Newport. She still had a key to the salon and she took me there on our last evening for a kiss and a cuddle. She had, unfortunately, been transferred to a training depot in the mainland, but she promised to keep in touch.

Before the war I was much involved in athletics. I was quite a good miler at club standard. I continued with my training whenever the circumstances permitted, running along the beach at Ryde at every opportunity. I had also trained regularly on the beach near Cowes, when I was stationed at Parkhurst, so when it was announced that there was to be an Army sports day at Fareham, on the mainland near Portsmouth, I put my name down for the mile and the half-mile.

There was a large entry for the mile, always the favourite event. Several of the other areas had a number of entrants, but I was the only representative from the Island.

I had earlier won the half mile, in a very close finish and I knew that the runners in that event, who were also participating in the mile, would be out to see that I did not repeat my success in the longer distance.

When the race started, it soon became apparent that some of the runners were trying to make it awkward for me and I was nearly run off the track. However, I managed to pull ahead on the last bend and won, once again, in an exciting finish.

The senior officer, who had come down specially from London to present the prizes said, when I appeared for my third prize – I had also taken part in a successful relay race – 'Not you again!' I saw him later, talking to my new commanding officer. A short time afterwards I was told to report to the colonel in Newport, who informed me that I was being recommended for a commission.

Just when things seemed to be looking up, there came a terrible blow. News reached me that my elder brother, who was a navigator in the RAF, had been killed when landing in a Wellington bomber, somewhere in the Midlands. The runway had been damaged by bombing and not adequately repaired. We were extremely fond of each other. Tragically, he need not have joined the forces, as he was in a reserved occupation. He was a very gifted artist and spent some time at the Slade school of Art. His instructor one day said to him that there was nothing more he could teach him. Sadly, all his paintings and drawings were destroyed in an air raid.

IV: *Hilda*

I woke up suddenly to the familiar sound of an exploding bomb. The dull thud shook the bed in which I had been sleeping, It was not at the Ryde depot, as I had finished very late the previous evening, distributing rations to the multitude of troops which had crossed over to the Island from the mainland under the cover of darkness and I had been given accommodation in another Army camp.

The troops had arrived by landing craft and had been spirited away to various tamps in different parts of the Island. One group, however, was billeted in an old castle, which received a direct hit, but fortunately the thick walls of the battlements withstood most of the blast and the casualties were light. The bombing hadn't been severe and the most disturbing aspect was the apparent awareness of the Germans of this supposedly secret troop movement. Only a few days previously there had been rumours of a woman being apprehended at Niton after she was detected sending out Morse code signals.

There were Canadian soldiers, British soldiers, including crack regiments of Guards and men from Commando units; also, there were men and officers from the U.S. Rangers Regiment. Distributing food to them was a major operation.

In Newport, before it was placed off limits, groups of Guardsmen and Commandos met for pitched battles in the town square. I once saw a guardsman being hurled bodily through the plate glass window of a shop by an enormous commando. The local populace had all disappeared into their homes. The soldiers were just letting off steam.

For a few days, early in August, 1942, these troops were allowed to relax. They could have had no idea what was in store for them.

The girls on the Island, including some members of the women's services, were only too happy to befriend the men and many relationships were struck up during the short time of their stay.

I, too, became friendly with a few of them whom I had met during the course of distributing rations. They sometimes came with me in the evening, to a restaurant in Gurnard, near Cowes, using my truck. Often we would have a swim, the weather at that time being very warm.

The chaps usually brought some girls with them and we had an enjoyable time in the restaurant. One of the girls was an accomplished pianist and she would accompany us with a variety of cheerful songs. I became very friendly with her and I used to see her privately for a swim and a meal and would then drive her back to Newport.

We became very attached and saw each other frequently. We would often meet at Gurnard and sit together on a bench at the bus stop. She would come by bus.

The buses didn't run very late and as it was the end of the route, we were not disturbed. It was a pleasant spot, overlooking the sea and surrounded by trees.

Hilda was a small, very lively person and very passionate. She tried to encourage me to make love to her, but I always managed to resist. It wasn't easy, but I always had in mind the mistake my brother had made when his girlfriend became pregnant and he had married her, knowing that they were not compatible. He never said so, but I was always convinced that he had joined the R.A.F. to escape the unhappy situation, when he could have continued in his occupation as a craftsman.

I thought at the time that it was rather strange that Hilda never invited me to see her parents, who lived in Newport. The reason became apparent when I discovered that she was engaged to a chap who worked on the mainland in a reserved occupation, although it seemed that her girlfriends, who we occasionally met, were well aware of the situation. I felt very let down.

When I questioned Hilda, she admitted that she had deceived me, but said that she was very much in love with me and proposed to call off her engagement, if I would promise to continue to see her. She added that she had only agreed to marry her fiancé to please her parents and was glad that he did not work on the Island and only visited her occasionally.

I suppose I was gullible. This was my first affair and men are easily manoeuvred in this kind of situation, especially when away from home and in need of affection. So I continued to see her.

Very soon the troops were on their way to carry out a probing exercise to test the effectiveness of the German defences on the French coast at Dieppe.

This was the brainchild of Churchill, supported by Admiral Lord Louis Mountbatten. It was to be a 'reconnaissance in force' to use Churchill's words 'to test the enemies defences'. 'Somewhere, at some time, the re-conquest of the Continent must begin with the first British or American soldier wading ashore out of the sea' had said historian John Ehrman. It was probable, also, that the frustration of the Canadian troops, who had by then been in the U.K. for several months, contributed to the decision to carry out the operation. It was code-named 'Jubilee'.

Tragically, it soon became apparent, after the forces had arrived off Dieppe, that the whole enterprise had been ill-conceived, the intelligence had been poor and the ignorance of the strength of the enemy defences and their true disposition proved to be catastrophic.

Time and tide had dictated the last date in 1942 suitable for the operation, as being August 18th. Tank landing craft, totalling twenty-four in all embarked Churchill tanks under the cover of smoke.

The total force comprised over six thousand officers and men and they boarded their landing craft. There were sixty squadrons of fighter aircraft for support, mostly Spitfires and seven squadrons of bombers and fighter-bombers. The destroyer escort carried four-inch guns.

The afternoon of August 18th saw the final clearance by minesweepers.

On the night of the 18th approximately two hundred and fifty ships sailed from four ports – infantry landing craft, eight destroyers, a sloop and numerous assault and landing craft. In wireless silence and in almost total darkness they departed, arriving undetected eight miles off Dieppe at about 0300 hours on the morning of the 19th.

The ships took up battle stations with destroyer HMS *Calpe*, the headquarters ship and the attendant destroyer HMS *Fernie*. The remaining six destroyers fanned out to act as lookouts for the force and to support the attackers.

One group had a task reminiscent of the days of Sir Francis Drake. Seven Free French chasseurs, led by the Royal Navy gunboat *Locust*, were to attempt to rush Dieppe harbour, seize forty enemy invasion barges and tow them back to England as a prize.

The orders for the rest of the force were to seize Dieppe and the vicinity and. to occupy the area until demolition and exploitation had been carried out and then to return to England.

About one thousand officers and men of Number Three and Number Four Royal Marine Commandos, with the fifty officers of the U.S. Rangers had supporting roles. Also taking part were the Essex Scottish Regiment, the Royal Hamilton Light Infantry, The Royal Regiment of Canada, the South Saskatchewan Regiment and the Queen's Own Cameron Highlanders of Canada, who were to capture the fortified position known as 'Les Quatre Vents' farm and take the west headland in the rear.

Troops would also move through the river Scie valley to capture St Aubin airfield and the headquarters of the German division at Arques la Battaille.

The support on the Dieppe beaches would be supplied by the 14th Canadian Army Tank Battalion.

At 0300 hours the infantry landing ships lowered their landing craft. The Commandos on the outer flanks were already moving behind their leading gunboats and by 0330 hours, five thousand men were in their assault landing craft, taking stations behind the gunboats which would lead them in to land.

At that time all was well.

At 0347 hours gunfire erupted at sea on the left flank, Disaster had overtaken the gunboat leading in Number Three Commando, for without warning it had almost run into a group of five armed enemy trawlers. A star shell illuminated the scene and in less than ten minutes the gunboat was virtually destroyed.

One landing craft of the group managed to land three officers and seventeen men and this small group, armed only with their personal weapons and one 2-inch mortar, so harassed one of the German garrisons that it prevented them from firing into the main target area during the landing.

On the right flank at the same time Number Four Commando destroyed a German battery and before 0730 hours had departed on their return journey to England, their mission completed.

But this was almost the only success of the operation. An hour after the assaults, intense fire from the headland and accurate shelling of the assault area from behind the beaches told a dismal story. The guns of the British destroyers and the attacks of the fighter-bombers failed to make much impression.

The leading troops had pushed on to their objectives, but were unable to sustain their attacks without armour and without help from the Dieppe beaches, which was not forthcoming. The Royal Regiment of Canada was almost annihilated. They were late in landing and were caught in the beams of a searchlight. In a few minutes the regiment was reduced to less than two companies, who were pinned down.

Of their 27 officers and 516 men, just three officers and 57 men were eventually rescued from the beach.

The remainder, with men of the Black Watch, The Royal Canadian Artillery, the beach parties and the navel crews of the landing and support craft, died on the shore, or were marched off to prison camps.

Of the twenty-four tank landing craft, ten managed to land a total of twenty-eight tanks, all of which were lost. Like the men, few of them managed to get off the beach.

"The attempt to seize Dieppe had foundered in the shallows and died on the beaches" – to quote historian R.W. Thompson.

It is not generally known that perhaps the greatest air battle of the war, carried out in a single day, was fought over Dieppe at this time.

The main task of the Royal Air Force was, of course, to provide support for the landings, but at the same time they wanted to entice the Luftwaffe into the air to destroy it.

It was not until 1000 hours that the enemy appeared in strength, at which time the forces were endeavouring to withdraw from the beaches.

Between 1010 hours and 1040 hours, while fully engaged against enemy fighters and bombers, Bostons and Hurricanes made ferocious assaults on the headland and these, together with the Blenheims, went repeatedly in support of the ground troops.

By 1300 hours, the R.A.F. had triumphed. Not one enemy bomber had succeeded in attacking the landing craft or any of the shipping, but this tremendous effort was to no avail.

The R.A.F. flew 2617 sorties for the loss of 106 aircraft, including 88 Spitfires. The enemy admitted to 170 losses. In the air, at least, that day, it was a victory.

Throughout the battle the air-sea rescue launches carried out their rescue missions, in the maze of assault craft and shipping.

Some thirteen pilots and one observer were rescued, at a cost of eleven officers and twenty-six men, killed, wounded or missing.

Shortly afterwards a few of the Canadians who had survived returned to the Island. They included two of those I had met previously and I heard their personal account of the horrific experience they had undergone.

They were convinced, that the Germans had been alerted to the attack and had been waiting for them. They were members of the Royal Regiment of Canada and they had been trapped on the beach. Their unloading ramp had stuck halfway down and they had to leap over it to reach the shoreline. They managed to scramble to the sea wall for cover but the following men were cut down by machine-gun fire.

They were unable to move forward or to retreat and they could only watch while the guns of the German batteries engaged the ships offshore. Shells burst continuously on the beach and bodies lay everywhere, among the shattered landing craft and burning tanks.

Not many men were rescued from the beaches. The tide had receded and the water's edge by midday was 100 yards from the sea wall, behind which they had huddled all morning. They somehow made it to one of the few landing craft still afloat, which had come in to take survivors. It was laden with wounded soldiers. Despite the heavy shelling and continuous machine-gun fire, it had managed to pull away to safety.

The whole affair had been a nightmare for them and they had been given two week's leave to recuperate. Over half of their comrades had perished.

To end on a more cheerful note, one of these two Canadians, who had befriended a girl on his earlier visit to the Island, proposed to her and I was privileged to attend their wedding in a small church near Cowes.

I was summoned to Army Headquarters in Winchester to be interviewed by a General Officer, for him to decide whether or not. I was 'officer material'. It was something of an ordeal, not that I was worried about the interview, but some time earlier I had been at Gurnard with Hilda and we were having fun, chasing each other along the promenade, after we had had a swim and she swung around a post and we collided, resulting in me sustaining a very badly swollen ankle.

Hilda helped me back to the Army hospital in Parkhurst; I had to leave the truck as I couldn't drive and so we travelled by bus.

I spent the next two weeks in bed, which was something of an ordeal, alleviated to some extent the kind attention I received from the nurses. The hospital backed on to the supply store and as soon as I was sufficiently mobile, I went down the hospital fire escape at the rear and collected a few extra food supplies for them.

I wrote to Hilda but omitted to add 'Isle of Wight' to the Newport address, which I had thought unnecessary as I was on the Island, but the letter was sent to Newport in Monmouthshire and of course Hilda didn't receive it; she thought that I was cross with her as she had caused the collision which injured my ankle. Of course, I wasn't annoyed with her, but it was sometime before I could see her to tell her so.

When I travelled to Winchester for the interview, my ankle was still swollen and painful and walking along the cobbled streets was an agonizing experience. However, I managed to show a brave face to the general and it was not long before I was on my way to London to undergo the ordeal of a War Office Selection Board.

This consisted of a three-day capability test, when potential officers were put under constant surveillance to determine their suitability, or otherwise, for a cadet training course. Even at meal times, the resident officers mingled with us, I suppose to see whether we knew how to conduct ourselves properly at the table.

We were engaged in several exercises, when, alternately, each of us had to take over as leader of the squad. I soon learned that the examining officers were impressed with physical fitness. I had my athletic training behind me – and the willingness to assist the less active participants when they fell back over the obstacles. After my month with the Durham Light Infantry I found the obstacle courses easy going. Even running round the quarter-mile, track, carrying a heavy load, did not distress me. The tactical exercises I enjoyed, despite my lack of infantry training.

On the last evening we had to put on an impromptu variety show in the small theatre. Fortunately, one of the chaps had had some stage experience.

I appeared in one sketch as an officer and I think I gave quite a good performance. In another sketch I took the part of an absent-minded doctor. The scene was in a hospital ward. Two nurses were tucking up a patient who had just returned from surgery and were discussing the surgeon's absent-mindedness.

"Only yesterday," one of them said, "he left behind a scalpel inside a patient after an operation." The patient in the bed looks agitated. The ward door opens and the doctor enters. The nurses and the patient look at him.

"Has anyone seen my umbrella?" he asks.

The patient faints.

One of the chaps I had made friends with, a huge Scot known as Tiny, was left right to the end to do his bit. He had only a few minutes before the show was due to end. He entered on stage alone and said, "Ladies and Gentlemen, I am going to talk about sex." There was a nervous rustle in the audience, which was comprised of the staff, their wives and some visiting senior officers. "Ladies and Gentlemen," he repeated, "it gives me great pleasure..." After saying this, he turned and walked off!

I returned to the depot in Ryde to await events. It was not long before a notice appeared on the board stating that I had been accepted for admission to the officer cadet-training unit in Wrotham, in Kent, not far from my home.

I was soon bidding farewell to my colleagues and to Hilda. She told me that she had given up her fiancé and wanted to visit me in London when I was able to get time off from my training. I was very fond of her, although still feeling rather hurt at the way she had deceived me, but I told her that I would be very pleased to see her in London when I could get time off. In the event, she never did come up to see me; I gathered that her parents had raised objections. It appeared that they still dominated her. I had never been given the opportunity to meet them.

Arriving at Wrotham, I was soon to discover that becoming an officer was going to be something of an ordeal. In fact, quite a number of the men on the course gave up and went back to their units.

Right from the start it was made clear that for the three months of our stay we were going to be regarded as very inferior human beings. We were stripped of all rank – I had been merely a sergeant, but there were a number of senior warrant officers. They must have found it especially hard, as some of the instructors had only the rank of sergeant or corporal and seemed to have been chosen especially for their unpleasant demeanour.

The chief drill instructor, a Coldstream Guards sergeant major, was able to strike real terror in the hearts of all of us. Practising the slow march under his instruction was a particularly awesome experience.

The weather, again, was filthy and we were billeted in the dreaded Nissen huts. It was now winter and it snowed quite a lot. The huts were freezing and caked ice would form down the centre, brought in by the Army boots.

We were required to smarten ourselves for parades to quite a ridiculous extent, considering the weather and the poor accommodation. The parade ground was a quagmire, but still we had to clean and polish our boots, although by the time we had negotiated the duck boards and trodden through the snow and mud, only a small patch of our highly polished boots, was visible on the toes when we finally arrived at the ground. On the few days when it was dry, we were required to polish the steel studs on our boots and to make sure that none of them was missing.

We were not allowed to Blanco our equipment in the hut and so, when we came off duty, after a hard day's grind of exercises and lectures, we could be seen under the dripping trees, in the dark and bitter cold, cleaning our equipment by torch-light. It sounds ridiculous, but quite true.

Wrotham was not very far away from my home, as the crow flies and although we were strictly forbidden to venture home on our infrequent days off, I could not resist the opportunity, but it was a long walk to the station to catch the train to Bromley, where I had to change trains for Petts Wood, my hometown.

I had to take great care as I would have been in serious trouble, had I been apprehended without a pass; all chances of a commission would have disappeared.

The end of the course was approaching and I seemed to be surviving it. We were on another of the interminable, exercises, having been on an assault course and now lying on the wet grass, in our battle gear, on the rifle range, filthy, sweating and tired.

I was about to take aim on the target when I received a tap on the shoulder and was instructed to report immediately to the company office. There I was told to leave my rifle and to await a call into the next room.

I began to wonder what it was about – perhaps I was to be told off for some misdemeanour or other. Had they discovered that I had been going home on my day off? Was I about to be kicked out?

Soon I was marched next door and told to stand at ease. At a large table, facing me, sat about half a dozen officers, two of senior rank, all of them with deep suntans. One of them had a huge walrus moustache, which reminded me of the legendary Colonel Blimp. This officer eyed me up and. down for a while, no doubt taking in my filthy, sweat-stained condition and then spoke.

"We have been examining your army record and we have decided that we would like you to come to India to complete your training with a view to becoming an officer in the Indian Army. What do you think of the idea?"

I thought for a moment.

"Yes sir," I replied, "I quite like the idea."

"Very good," he said. "You have the choice, either of being seconded from the British Army or of being discharged and enlisting in the Indian Army as an Indian national. If you make this second choice, however, you must realize that India would then be regarded as your home country and you would not be entitled to leave in the United Kingdom. We will be here until the end of the week and you have until then to make up your mind. You will, of course, receive embarkation leave, two weeks."

I was then dismissed and returned to the range.

I had made my decision before the end of the week. What had decided me to take the second option, of joining the Indian Army as a national, was simply that I had learned that the pay of a lieutenant was almost equal to that of a major in the British Army. The substantial extra money would enable me to make my mother a much more generous allowance.

I was not sorry to leave Wrotham for my two week's leave. It had been more of an ordeal than the period under canvas with the Durham Light Infantry.

My mother was pleased to see me again, but concerned about my imminent departure for India. She was still recovering from the shock of my brother's death. I felt rather guilty, having so readily agreed to join the Indian Army, but it was too late to reconsider.

I wrote at length to Hilda, to tell her the news. I promised to write to her regularly from India and I told her that if she still felt the same way about me on my return, I would be very happy to marry her.

At the end of my leave, I left for London. My mother was tearful on my departure and I felt very sad. I reported, as instructed, to the Great Eastern Hotel, where a group of us were being mobilized for the journey to India. We had no idea how long we were to be there and once more I managed a trip home. My mother was not greatly surprised to see me and when I left, for what really was the last time, our farewell was quite casual.

We left at night by train for Glasgow; we did not actually know it was Glasgow until we disembarked at the railway station. Everything was very secretive.

Soon we were on board the MV *Georgic*, which was to take us to Bombay and we were told that she would be forming part of a convoy, the first through the Mediterranean for about three years. There remained a risk from German submarines.

The next day we sailed. It was January the 9th, my birthday. I wondered what was in store for me and whether I would ever see my mother, Hilda or England again.

V: *Bombay Bound*

It is traditional in the British Army to treat officer cadets as being of no account whatever. My time at Wrotham had taught me this. At every turn, one is subjected to indignities. It came as no surprise, therefore, when I was instructed to mount guard in one of the gangways, with rifle and full equipment.

I had no idea what I was supposed to be guarding. All I did know was that I was feeling terribly sick. The vessel was by now in the Irish Sea, not the calmest of waters in January. The ship was heaving and jarring and occasionally the propeller would come out of the water and everything shook violently.

Holding my rifle for support, I slowly sank to the deck, where I collapsed in a heap. Just then, the ship's captain, accompanied by the colonel in charge of troops and several other officers, appeared, doing an inspection. I was quite unable to rise to my feet to pay my respects.

"I hope we are not boarded by the enemy," was all the colonel said as the party stepped over me and proceeded on their way.

I had thought that going through the Mediterranean would have been much less of an ordeal, but I was surprised to find that, far from being blue, it was murky and extremely rough. I have always been a bad sailor; even travelling the two or three miles from Portsmouth to Ryde was an ordeal, unless the sea was very calm. This was the first sea voyage of any length I had experienced.

Great care was being taken to ensure that the convoy moved as discreetly as possible through the Med, to avoid contact with enemy shipping. There was a large notice, which we read as soon as we emerged from below decks: 'Nothing to be thrown overboard during daylight hours' – any floating debris would help to give the convoy's presence away. Somebody had added a word to the notice so that it read 'It's nothing to be thrown overboard during daylight hours' I thought it quite hilarious, as it echoed our feelings.

My first contact with an Arab occurred just after we had cleared the Suez Canal. The locals were offering articles for sale in their small bumboats and some were hauled on board so that we could make purchases. A particularly scruffy Arab emerged, very dark and oily looking; he regarded me for a few moments, rubbing his hands. I expected incomprehensible utterance from him; instead, he muttered "F—ing cold, ain't it?"

I was told later by a soldier who had served in Suez that the Arabs picked up these expressions from the troops stationed there.

Going through the Red Sea was an even worse experience. The weather was fine and hot, but since we were below decks, crammed tight like cattle, sleeping in bunks or hammocks, with very little air, the portholes being closed, the atmosphere was putrid.

Chaps were being sick all the time, sometimes vomiting when they were lying in a hammock, all over the occupant of a bunk underneath.

One night I could stand it no longer, went up on deck and slept on one of the bulkheads. I was awoken early in the morning by some sailors who were washing down the decks. When they had finished, I returned to the bulkhead and dozed off again. I awoke in broad daylight to find the decks teeming with personnel from most of the services, including Wrens and nurses, who were very amused by my presence, clad as I was in only a brief pair of shorts. I jumped off the bulkhead and made for the lower deck. Fortunately, no one in authority appeared to have seen me...

Those of us who were joining the Indian Army were required to attend Urdu lessons, given by an Indian Army captain. The language, I found, in the Roman version, was not too difficult, particularly as there are no irregular verbs. The infinity of every verb ends in 'na', which you knock off to leave the root and then add to this the bit that determines the tense and so on.

The construction of a sentence, in fact, depends not only on the tense, but also on to whom you are speaking, whether an equal, a superior or an inferior. This applies throughout the Indian subcontinent. Caste is everything.

It was a great relief when we finally docked at Bombay. The weather was fine and warm and it was a pleasure to feel the sun on my face as I walked with my companions down the gangway.

We proceeded to Victoria station, resembling nothing like the station of the same name in London, where we boarded a train taking us to Belgaum, not far from Poona, where we were to spend the next six months in training.

It was my first experience of Indian trains; there were no windows and the seats were wooden benches, covered with dust. But the journey through the countryside was enjoyable after the life aboard the *Georgic*. There appeared to be more passengers outside the carriages than inside; they clung precariously to the handrails and anything else they could hang on to.

I learned later that this was the accepted mode of transport for the poorer classes, as they could not afford the fare to travel from one village to another and the authorities did little to stop it.

We arrived at Belgaum station, where we disembarked and assembled on the platform. We were immediately jostled by passengers anxious to get on board the train before it pulled out. Trains did not seem to stop very long and this one was shrieking it's intention to depart without delay.

Nobody seemed to be paying much attention to us; probably by this time the locals were used to seeing pale-faced Eng-lishmen arriving en route to the academy.

We piled into the buses waiting to take us to our final destina-tion; these also were very ramshackle. They were not the property of the academy, I heard, but were hired from the local contractor.

We passed through Belgaum village, consisting mainly of small shops, all displaying their wares outside, leather goods, pottery and brassware; also wooden bowls trays and. boxes. The buses crawled through the village, dodging the populace and the buffaloes, who appeared to be wandering aimlessly as if they had no destination. One enormous buffalo had a young girl in charge of it – she was probably no more than six years old – who wielded a stick with which she struck the beast on it's hindquarters to send it in her chosen direction.

The vendors sat outside their shops, chattering incessantly. They hardly seemed to give the convoy of buses a glance, probably having no idea why we were travelling through their village and not caring very much. The war to them, assuming they even knew that there was one in progress, was so remote as not to be worthy of their concern.

The academy was a large, sprawling affair, consisting mainly of huts. Two of us were allocated to each of these and we shared a manservant, known as a bearer, whose duty it was to attend to the cleaning of the inside of the hut and to our laundry and the preparation of our breakfast – *chota hazri*.

Our meals were taken in a mess hall, where we sat on long wooden benches and ate off long tables, somewhat reminiscent of the early days at Parkhurst, but it would be doing an injustice to compare; everything was spotlessly clean and there were tablecloths and vases of flowers.

We were let off lightly with duties on the first day, just a couple of lectures about how we should behave towards the local populace and on bargaining in the bazaars. It is just not done to pay the asking price for an article; the shopkeepers do not expect it and would probably be very surprised and disappointed if you did not haggle.

On the second day, we sat down to a lunch of curry and rice, after a morning of strenuous exercise. We had each been given a large plate of steaming hot rice and the mess bearers were moving between us with large tureens of boiling hot curry, ladling it out as they proceeded. You can picture the scene; rows of tables and occupied benches, close to each other.

I was seated next to Pete Tansey, a fair-skinned, blonde young man from the Midlands, a very cheerful and pleasant sort of chap. He had played football for a professional team before the war. One of the chaps at the table behind us, turned to say something to a friend at our table, just as the bearer reached us with the curry and in doing so caused the bearer to upend the contents of the tureen over Pete's head.

Peter screamed in agony and someone had the presence of mind to pour a jug of water over him. He spent several weeks in hospital, having lost a lot of skin from his body. His eyesight also was badly affected.

We continued with our Urdu lessons, each of us having a *munshi* and I was lucky enough to have one who was an authority, having written several books on the language. It was from him I learnt that several of the words in Urdu come from Arabic; also, I remember him telling me why Muslims do not eat pork. It is because pigs cohabit indiscriminately and do not have a regular partner.

We had been told that after we were commissioned, assuming we passed the six-month course, no promotion would be possible unless we passed the Urdu examinations, written and oral; also, we understood, that when we passed, our tuition fees would be refunded to us. Promotion and the prospect of having our fees paid were considerable incentives to work hard to master the language.

The course consisted of lectures on battle tactics and jungle warfare, weapon training, public speaking and physical training, with the emphasis on the last of these. Each morning before breakfast, as the sun-rose, we went on parade in gym kit, when we were put through the most intensive exercises I had ever known. We were drilled to the point of exhaustion, but how wonderfully fit we became! It was marvellous to be able to run up a hill and to arrive at the crest without feeling the slightest distress. Everybody gave up smoking.

One of the instructor's favourite exercises was to have us run up Musketry Hill, which was barren and strewn with small rocks and then turn and run down again.

Assault courses were a daily routine and it was something of a miracle that we all managed to survive them. Our instructor had been the middleweight boxing champion of the British Army and was as tough as they come.

We had a sports day and with my usual enthusiasm for anything athletic I entered for several of the track events, including the hundred yards race, although this was not really my scene, being a middle distance runner. The weather was by now very warm and the grass on the track had long since disappeared. The ground was cracked with the heat and as hard as concrete.

We wore just shorts and shoes, mine being tennis shoes which I also wore as house slippers and the backs had been trodden down. Just as I leaped forward at the start of the hundred-yard dash, one of the shoes came off and I fell forward, landing on both knees, both elbows and on my chest and I slid along the ground.

I had sustained extensive grazing on all five points of contact and was covered with dust. Blood trickled down my chest.

We were next due to go on a ten-mile cross-country run, taking in Musketry Hill. I reported to the drill instructor with my wounds, confident that he would send me to the surgery for treatment. However, he decided that it would do me good to go on the run as, he said, sweating would help to cleanse the wounds.

I turned away to join the others and then he called me back and, uncharacteristically, relented and told me to go to the surgery; but I decided to go on the run. He was probably right, the sweat did help to cleanse the wounds, although I will not pretend that it was not an agonizing experience, especially when I tripped over again going up the hill and gashed a knee on one of the rocks.

From then on, the instructor and I became great friends and I sometimes went running with him in the evenings, when he was planning a route for one of the exercises.

He could not understand why I did not wish to join one of the crack infantry regiments or the Ghurkhas instead of the

Service Corps, which I had belonged to in England and which I intended to join when I was commissioned. That is, The Royal Indian Army Service Corps. Having spent four years in supplies and transport, it seemed rather foolish for me to waste the experience I had gained, having in mind that the war would probably not last much longer.

We had one day off each week and I usually went pony riding with one or other of the chaps. The poor animals were not very well treated by their owners and we used to feed them up with any odd scraps of food we could find. On one occasion, the pony I was riding was very lethargic and I persuaded my companion to allow me to ride his mount for a while. Just as I alighted, my pony swung around and lashed out with its hind legs, hitting my right thigh. I collapsed, in terrible pain.

My friend draped me over the back of his pony and proceeded to the sick bay with the two animals and myself. Fortunately for me, my thigh had caught just the end of the kick and the bone was not damaged, but for the next few weeks I was in considerable pain. It did not help matters when I fell down a slit trench during one of the exercises. I had not been excused any duties – we were expected to be tough.

We were not in any way restricted in our movements when we were off duty and since the shops and other establishments in the village stayed open all the evening and much of the night, we would often wander down there in the small hours of the morning, when the heat made sleeping difficult (there was not, of course, any air conditioning).

It was a novelty to get one's haircut at two o'clock in the morning, being served at the same time with a cup of tea. My Urdu was progressing quite well and I was soon able to hold a conversation, although hesitant, with the shopkeepers.

On one occasion I got into conversation with a very old man, sitting outside a shop, who told me that he had been to his son's wedding that morning. This puzzled me, as I could remember speaking to him before, when he informed me that his son lived about two hundred miles away. I asked him how he could have travelled such a distance and back, in one day, since he was infirm and clearly in no condition to travel very far. He gave me a smile and said that he was, of course, only there in spirit.

It took some time to understand that he had retired into a hut at the rear of the compound, where he had sat in darkness and meditated for a long time, until he felt that his spirit had left him and travelled to his son's house. Not only was he able to tell me who was there and about the activities, but he also knew that those present were aware of his presence.

He told this to me in a matter of fact way and it obviously did not occur to him that I might disbelieve his story.

I later mentioned the conversation to my Urdu teacher, a Hindu, who said that this ability to project the spirit was not a rare phenomenon in India, especially among the yogis, who practice meditation continuously.

There are, he added, seven levels of consciousness the seventh being perfection, never achieved by mortal man. He knew of a Brahmin, a member of the higher of the Hindu classes, who was able to understand any spoken language, although he had never had any language tuition.

Clearly, there are more things on earth than we dream of in our philosophies!

Before leaving for India, when working on the Isle of Wight, I frequently met a sergeant, in the course of issuing rations, who used facial makeup and had lacquered fingernails. I accepted this as being just a fad. He was a charming fellow. It was only when I came to India that I began to comprehend what homosexuality was about.

Two of the cadets at the academy would walk around arm in arm and were constantly in each other's company. This in itself was not extraordinary, but sometimes in the mess hall they would have tiffs, just like a married couple. They were billeted together in one of the huts. One of them was a well-known caricaturist, who still draws for a newspaper, the other a previous member of a Guards regiment.

The first of them, small and slim, was a marvellous athlete and I greatly admired him, despite his odd behaviour.

We were told one day that there was to be a parade for a visiting general and were warned that our turnout would have to be especially smart. The day arrived and it was terribly hot. We waited on the parade ground for what seemed like hours, several of the cadets collapsing in the heat, although strangely enough they were nearly all Indians; at this time they were being introduced into the King's commissioned ranks; previously they were allowed to hold only Viceroy commissions.

One of the white cadets who supposedly passed out had suddenly realized that he had forgotten to replace the bolt in his rifle when cleaning it; he had feigned illness so that he would be carried off and the missing bolt not discovered when we presented arms to the general. He could have been in serious trouble.

Eventually the general arrived for the inspection. It was General Aukinlek, 'the Auk' as we had known him at Wilton House. He was now the Commander-in-Chief of the Indian forces. As he appeared, ready to inspect the first line of cadets, the band struck up with the Colonel Bogey march, which everyone who has been in the British Army will know, has had some very vulgar words added to it. It was obvious that the general also knew these unseemly words, as his face broke into a smile as he neared me.

The terrible performance of the band, completely out of tune, made it all the more amusing.

The general looked quizzically at me as he approached and said, "I have seen you before somewhere."

"At Wilton House," I replied.

"Of course. How are you getting on here?"

"I am enjoying the course, General."

He smiled as he moved on; such a nice chap. He was not to know that I had made good use of his bath until apprehended.

Half way through the course we were allowed three day's leave to visit Bombay, having been warned that the red light district was strictly out of bounds. This made us all the more determined to visit it. I was accompanied by Pete Tansey, who had almost recovered from his ordeal by curry. His face had taken on a pink aspect, not brown like the rest of us and he wore dark spectacles continually, but his spirits were as high as ever. He had recently been told off by the Academy commandant for playing football, barefooted, with some of the Indian servants. He was something of a rebel.

We stayed at the Taj Mahal Hotel, named after the temple in Agra; it was fronted by large palm trees, swaying in the breeze blowing off the Arabian Sea. The trees helped to hide a curious aspect of the hotel. The front, with its impressive entrance, was at the rear, overlooking a dingy street, strewn with rubbish, and the back of the hotel, with large windows allowing a view into the kitchen, which faced the promenade.

We were told that the hotel had been designed by an Italian architect who came to see the building after its completion. When he saw that it had been constructed the wrong way round he committed suicide by jumping off the parapet.

We did not venture into the sea for a swim, there being a very attractive bathing pool nearby, called Breach Candy, where we spent much of our time.

Of course we were curious to visit the red light district, which proved to be a very sordid area; dimly lit in the evening by oil lamps. Young girls beckoned to us through barred windows, but although sexually deprived, we did not fancy risking our health in the arms of one of these damsels, although this view was not shared by at least one officer, who we saw emerging from one of the establishments.

Call girls frequented the bar and the lobby of the hotel. The barman recounted to us an incident told to him by one of the girls. An officer had arrived at the hotel on leave with his wife and while she was getting herself ready for dinner, he had come down to the bar to await her arrival. A girl approached him and he asked her "how much?"

"A hundred rupees," she said.

"I'll give you fifty," he responded, at which she turned away. Just then the wife descended the stairs and the officer joined her and they proceeded to the dining room, passing the girl on the way, who whispered to the officer, "See what you get for fifty rupees!"

We spent the last day of our vacation wandering around the bazaars and visiting places of interest. The ghats on the outskirts of the town were interesting. They were square buildings with iron bars in place of a ceiling, on which dead bodies of Brahmins we placed so that the scavenger birds, kite hawks, could eat the flesh, the bones then dropping through to the floor of the edifice, where they were buried.

My impression of Bombay, after our short visit, was a confused mixture of admiration for the industry of the people, the constant scurrying of tongas and bicycles, the smells in the bazaar and the prevailing humour of the inhabitants, many of whom lived in abject poverty, but always greeted one with a smile.

Two of the Indian cadets were Brahmins, the father of one of them owning substantial property in Bombay. They were both well educated and spoke with upper-class English accents.

Their family had adopted English names, one of them Brown, the other Cooper.

Despite their European outlook and mannerisms – Brown used English swear words quite freely – they still adhered to the customary rules of their caste.

I called to see Cooper one day and, although the weather was fine and hot, he had a fire burning in the grate and he was burning what transpired to be items of underwear.

When I asked him what he was doing, he explained that they were forbidden to allow anyone else to wear their clothing and he was obliged to dispose of it when it became worn.

"Bloody lot of nonsense," he said, as he poked the fire, "but if I threw it away, one of the servants would get hold of it."

He agreed that, although he considered it to be nonsense, together with the other restrictions imposed upon them, he would, no doubt, insist on his children conforming.

It was always a source of wonder to me that he had no time for Indian music, which he thought monotonous, but was very keen on western classical music, and was continually playing Brahms, Mozart and Chopin on some old gramophone records he had managed to find in the market, no doubt discarded by an officer returning to England. He had a dilapidated old gramophone, which constantly needed to be wound up. Being fond of classical music myself, I was happy to spend time with him, particularly as he clearly derived great pleasure from the performances. The records were not in very good condition and the needle was worn, but it was still very enjoyable.

A film crew arrived one day, to make a documentary about the Indian cadets and although some of us from England appeared briefly in the film, we were kept very much in the background.

It was plain that the film director was anxious to concentrate the interest on the Indian cadets, but they had not had very much army training at this time, and did not make a very good showing, especially when handling weapons. In fact, we had difficulty in containing our mirth on occasions. The director, who was from a studio in Bombay, became exasperated with some of their antics.

Sometime in January, soon after we arrived in Belgaum, it became very overcast and I said to the bearer that it looked like rain, in my then halting Urdu. He smiled and said, "No Sahib, not until April." Sure enough, the first rain fell on 2nd April and it poured incessantly for three days.

It does not rain very often in that part of the world, but when it does, it makes up for lost time. There were hailstones almost as large as golf balls, which thundered on the roofs and turned the ground white as if it had been snowing. Then on the third day it stopped and the hot sun came out again, steam rising from the ground.

Everything made of leather had green mildew on it, caused by the damp and the humidity. There not being any drainage and the roads not being made up, we had to walk around in the mud. But at least for a few days we were spared the rigours of the usual outdoor activities. We also had more time to concentrate on learning Urdu and to do other academic work.

Towards the end of the course we were taken on a day's outing to Goa, which is on the coast, not far from Belgaum. The contrast between Goa and what we had already seen of the rest of India was truly amazing. We were transported from the dust and the grimy streets to a place of supreme cleanliness and immaculate presentation There was little sign of the usual beggars and none of the aura of depression that seemed to permeate much of the Indian scene. Instead, there were smartly dressed, fresh looking, clear eyed natives, going about their business, in serene fashion.

Although very hot, the heat was much more tolerable, as the cool ocean breeze blew in our faces, after disturbing the branches of the large, swaying palm trees, weighted down by enormous coconuts, which lined the beach.

Gorgeous flowers of all kinds were in abundance, hibiscus and bougainvilleas created an atmosphere of charm and tranquillity. The sea gently lapped the shore; the beach of shimmering golden sand, stretching for miles, was a dream come true.

We ate our midday meal in a restaurant on the beach. It consisted mainly of seafood – prawns, lobster and tuna and then succulent mangoes.

We tried the local brew, made from cashew and coconut, drunk with lemon. It was very powerful and after our long spell of almost total abstinence – alcohol was forbidden at the: academy – we all became very heady, but relaxed and cheerful. The meal was prepared expertly and presented in great style.

Of course, this was not truly India. It was a Portuguese colony, taken over centuries before and the Portuguese had imported much of their culture and style, which was evidenced by the European appearance of most of the residences and the churches. Many of the inhabitants were Christians, we were told, converted by the Jesuit missionaries many years before.

We bathed in the warm sea and lay in the sun for the rest of the day, until the sun was about to set and then made our way reluctantly back to the transport which was to take us on our return journey to Belgaum.

Shortly before the end of our six months at the academy, the instructor made a special effort to arrange an assault course which was calculated 'to sort the men from the boys' as he had told me. It was exceptionally demanding and took in the crossing of the local river by ropes, slung across from bank to bank. One or two of the less robust cadets fell into the river and were swept some way down, but they were soon rescued and no one was seriously injured.

The following day we went on an exercise in the jungle, several miles from the academy. We managed to cover only about a mile during the course of the day, hacking our way through the undergrowth. We did not come across any tigers, as we had hoped, but we met up with a ferocious buffalo, which was awesome and scared us to death. We were armed and managed to ward it off with our rifles.

There was something quite marvellous, which impressed me profoundly. Dozens of butterflies appeared in the clearings, beautiful creatures, some of an enormous size. They alighted on our heads and on our extended arms and on our shoulders. They showed no signs of fear. This was their first contact with man and they had not learned to fear us, which is somehow rather sad.

We had to cross a small river and we were attacked by leeches, which found their way through the eye-holes in our boots to gorge themselves on our blood. It was difficult to remove them without leaving their jaws still embedded in our feet. The best way to deal with them, we discovered, was to apply a lighted cigarette, which encouraged them to withdraw themselves.

On the penultimate day of the course, we had to undergo battle inoculation. This included standing in trenches while machine guns were fired over our heads. Small tanks, loaned to the academy, were run over the trenches while we crouched in them. No one was injured except for one chap who had foolishly put his hand on the edge of the parapet and this was crushed.

A senior instructor took over to teach us the handling of hand grenades. There was a walled enclosure where each of us in turn was handed a grenade and told to remove the pin while holding firmly the lever that controlled the fuse. We then had to lob the grenade over the wall. Afterwards, when we were all assembled together, the instructor told us that grenades were not to be feared, if handled properly and to demonstrate this he took hold of a grenade, withdrew the pin and threw the grenade. Unfortunately, it struck a small tree and bounced back towards us. We threw ourselves to the ground and the only casualty was one of the chaps, who was hit in the bottom with some of the shrapnel and had to be carried off to the hospital.

It was left until the morning of the final day for us to take our Urdu tests. They were written and oral, the latter, for me, being the most difficult. It wasn't so much knowing the words as identifying them as they were spoken by a *havildar*, the Indian equivalent of a sergeant. I had some difficulty in understanding him. However, I managed to pass and was pleased to be refunded the fees I had paid to the *munshi*.

In the afternoon, we were paraded to be given our certificates of competence. At least, most of us did. It appeared that I had done quite well on the course and I was told that in view of my performance and of my previous experience in the British Army, I was to be granted the rank of full lieutenant.

We had the quite pleasant task of visiting the local tailor to be measured for our uniforms and greatcoats. We were given an allowance to pay for these.

The next few days were spent getting our kit packed, paying off any bills we had run up and having last minute discussions on Indian customs and the handling of Indian troops, many of whom, we were told, were quite illiterate, would probably have never worn footwear before joining the army and usually had great difficulty in adapting themselves to a military life.

In short, we had to be prepared to become father figures and not to expect the sort of discipline we had been used to with the soldiers in England. In return for our tolerance and understanding we would be rewarded with their total allegiance and devotion to duty. I looked forward to the challenge.

I was informed that I had been posted to a supply depot in Peshawar, on the North West Frontier, at the foot of the Khyber Pass, but before proceeding there I would be going on a further course for a month, at a place in the mountains called Kakul.

One morning in June we bade farewell to the Academy staff and to the servants and departed as commissioned officers to the next stage of our training. We had held a farewell party the previous evening.

We were moving off in all directions and unlikely to meet up again in India, but perhaps in England after the war. Three of the chaps, however, were also going to Kakul for the course, although I was the only one posted to Peshawar.

VI: The North West Frontier

The freshness of the mountain air of Kakul, was a welcome change to the heat and dust of Belgaum, but we were glad of our heavy overcoats, which had seemed to be an unnecessary accoutrement when we left the academy. Even so, they were not warm enough and were able to hire full-length fur coats for a few rupees a day.

On the first night, it snowed heavily and the snow lay at least a foot deep the following morning; more snow than I could ever recall experiencing at home.

The course began with the inevitable, lectures, but with more emphasis on the customs of the Indian people and their diverse religious beliefs, which dominate their social behaviour.

We were taught the detailed functioning of vehicle engines and transmission and the handling and maintenance of army vehicles.

The other practical aspect of the course was the organizing of convoys. These took us through mountain passes and way up above the clouds, traversing unmade roads onto which spewed rocks from the mountains, dislodged by the heavy snow, making driving hazardous through villages with exotic names such as Garihalibullakhen and Muzattarabad, and then down into the valleys.

I enjoyed this experience and I think I made an impression on the instructors with my knowledge of map reading and my ability to rendezvous with the convoy at a given location precisely at the given time.

We each took a turn in commanding a convoy, having a jeep with a driver to patrol as the vehicles proceeded.

The nearest place of any size was Abbottabad in the Black Mountains north of Rawlpindi, not far from Kashmir. Rawlpindi was the town in which the headquarters of the North West Frontier Army were located. Abbottabad was just a large village, with ramshackle shops and huts piled high on top of each other and one tiny hotel called the Ritz, the name being indicated on a large wooden plank which hung lopsidedly in front.

The melting of the snow in the mountains brought torrential streams of water cascading through the village; there were deep gulleys about two feet wide on each side of the roads, to take the deluge.

The academy boasted a very nice commissary, staffed by attractive girls from one of the services. There were dances on one evening each week, but as the men greatly outnumbered the women, most of the evening was spent waiting for a turn for a dance.

An exhilarating experience was climbing up in the mountains, high above the clouds, and looking down the deep ravines with the smell of pine trees and the glorious sunsets.

We were allowed a week's vacation after the course before joining our units; two of my colleagues from Belgaum and one other chap, Jim Coultard and I, decided to spend the time in Lahore.

We had been told that Lahore, being a fairly large town, had excellent hotels, with one in particular, Faletti's, being strongly recommended.

The transition from Kakul to the heat of Lahore, although only a hundred miles separated the two places, was quite staggering, the temperature being some fifty or sixty degrees higher. For a couple of days we felt quite bemused.

Faletti's hotel was indeed superb and very much appreciated after the sparse accommodation we had occupied for the previous seven months; we congratulated ourselves on the choice of Lahore for our holiday.

There were well-attended race meetings, riding stables and beautiful gardens. There were also some very nice restaurants, serving European food, my favourite dish being a mixed grill, which I ordered on a number of occasions but which I seldom managed to finish, as the portions were always so generous.

Arriving back at the hotel late one night, feeling tired and a little the worse for drink, I recall having a wash and sliding into bed, after divesting myself of my clothing and hanging my army jacket on a hook behind the door. The first thing I noticed when I awoke the next morning was the pocket flap of my jacket, which was loose and I realised that my money, which I kept in the pocket, had been stolen. Usually, when going to bed, I made a habit of removing the money and putting it under my pillow, but I had not done so on this occasion.

The remarkable thing was that the door squeaked quite loudly and there was also a *chowkidar* (a nightwatchman) who slept on a charpoy placed across the passageway leading to the bedrooms. I had heard nothing and neither had he. The thief must somehow have climbed over him without disturbing him, or perhaps squirmed under the bed; unless, of course, he was an accomplice.

The hotel manager was not very sympathetic; it was obvious that he was quite used to this sort of thing happening in the hotel. He said that I was fortunate I had not awoken, as the thieves invariably carried knives with them and I would have undoubtedly been stabbed to death.

I called round to see the manager of the local branch of Grindley's bank and he agreed to advance me some money to pay the hotel bill and for my travelling expenses to Peshawar.

The last day of our holiday arrived all too soon and as I had to catch an early train, my friends saw me off at the station. I had a carriage all to myself, which was luxuriously appointed – a far cry from the bare boards and windowless compartments of the train we took on our arrival in India.

The train stopped for a time at Rawalpindi (now Islamabad) where several other officers got aboard and they filled me in about life in Peshawar and the antics that the tribesmen from the hills got up to.

The journey, of around 400 miles, took about eight hours.

On arrival in Peshawar I reported to the adjutant at the brigade headquarters and after a short chat was shown into the office of the commander of the RIASC Supplies and Transport Division of the North West Frontier Army.

Colonel Shepherd was a very pleasant man, large and robust, with a twinkle in his eye, which I found very engaging. After the preliminary exchange of courtesies he told me that the supply depot in which I would be working, some three miles from the town, was currently under siege by Pathan tribesmen. They had come down from the hills, armed with rifles and had pinned down the sepoys within the walls surrounding the depot.

From the manner in which he informed me, I got the impression that he was not very concerned about the siege. He considered it good battle practice for the troops and he told me that the tribesmen would depart as soon as they became bored and ran out of food.

The object of the attack, the colonel said, was to obtain supplies from the depot, but he was confident that they would not succeed. They often made attempts, which were always frustrated. They sometimes climbed the high walls at night and occasionally succeeded in getting away with tins of ghee (clarified butter) and bags of lentils, but this was tolerated.

It was not easy for the Army to stop the Pathans from behaving in this fashion. The troops often made forays up the Khyber Pass, just outside Peshawar, where most of the tribesmen lived, but because of the terrain, the Pathans were able to ward off attacks, from strategic positions in the foothills, on either side of the Pass; it was not practical to use armoured vehicles. However, the Army considered it a useful way for the troops to become battle inoculated.

A concrete road had been constructed, to take vehicles up the Pass as far as Landi Kotel, which was a strategic point overlooking Afghanistan. There was always the fear that the Russians might decide to invade India through the Pass, as the country was vulnerable, with the greater portion of the Indian Army engaged in defending the Eastern borders against the Japanese.

The Pathans had provided much of the labour in the construction of the road and were paid quite well for their services. Their subsistence was at a low level, since they were not able to grow much food in the barren countryside and they relied heavily on revenue from the Army, who employed them for menial and labouring tasks, notwithstanding their attempt's to obtain food by force from the supply depot.

It was a rather strange world I was entering.

Most of the Pathan's weapons were stolen from the army or made from parts which somehow, found their way onto the local market. The depot guards had their rifles chained to their wrists to prevent them from being stolen, but it was not unknown for the tribesmen to attack them at night and hack off their hands to obtain their weapons.

It came as a severe blow to the tribesmen when the road was completed, as it had provided a steady income for several months, but not to be thwarted, during the night they brought down some heavy tools they had purloined from the stores and smashed up the road in several places.

There was no alternative but to employ them again to carry out the necessary repairs.

When this had been done and they came down a few nights later to smash the road up again, it created a difficult situation. Eventually, after much discussion and bargaining, it was agreed that the army would pay each Pathan twenty rupees a month to protect a stretch of the road.

From then on, the tribesmen could be seen at regular intervals, way up the Pass, sitting by the roadside, each guarding his own stretch of road.

Of course, their friends would not damage their stretch, knowing that if they did so they would be punished by the rest of the tribe for denying their comrade his monthly income; and so the scheme worked.

It was also agreed that if the Army, with their vehicles, kept to the road, the Pathans would not take pot shots at them, as they had been in the habit of doing.

I was taken by jeep, with my luggage, to my bungalow in the cantonment, this being the district occupied by the officers, some with wives and families and their servants.

The main thoroughfare was the Mall, a name commonly used in cantonments in India and no doubt derived from the street of the same name in London. The native population lived in the city, an entirely different place.

My quarters were very pleasant, nice and airy. Each room had a large overhead fan, which could be operated to revolve at various speeds. There was a spacious garden, including a badminton court; this pleased me greatly, as I had played the game for several years before joining the army. I had no doubt that there would be fellow officers to give me a game.

On top of the bungalow was a large water tank, heated by the sun during the day, providing plenty of hot water to the bathroom for a shower and for the *dhobi* to do the washing.

I was introduced to Raschid, who was to look after my requirements. He was a handsome man who, I understood, had two wives, although how he managed to keep both of them and their children on the few rupees he earned was always a source of amazement to me.

He had two small homes, I discovered, situated at the rear of the cantonment and he used to sleep in each of them on alternate nights. I could see him going off in one direction one evening and in the other the following evening. He never looked very happy, which seemed rather surprising, having two young women to sleep with. The reason for his unhappiness, he confided to me one day, was that they conspired against him. He never dared buy something for one of them without buying something of equal value for the other, or the neglected wife would make his life a misery.

Raschid knew no English, which was not a bad thing, since it helped to inspire me to persevere with my Urdu. I met his wives only on one occasion; they were shy, timid little things, or so they seemed to me. It was the occasion of Raschid's birthday and my visit was a very special concession. Normally the women are kept away from all men apart from their close relatives.

By the next morning, the Pathans had withdrawn from the supply depot precincts and I was able to proceed to the depot to meet the officer in charge, a major.

I was greeted warmly by the major, who told me that he had been awaiting my arrival with enthusiasm. He had not been able to leave the depot when it was under siege. I could tell from his breath, as he swayed towards me, that he must have spent much of the time consoling himself with liquor. His face was red and blotchy.

I was told later that he had served in Burma and had had a very bad time. He was cut off from the regiment and had spent two weeks alone in the jungle, surrounded by Japanese troops, hardly daring to move. It had rained heavily for most of the time and the hole in which he had been hiding half filled with water. He had been constantly tormented by leeches and he had only managed to survive by searching at night for edible vegetation.

After he was rescued, he was handed a letter from his wife, which had been posted some weeks earlier in England, telling him that she had decided to leave him and had gone off with another man, accompanied by their children.

Sadly, but perhaps not surprisingly, he had taken to the bottle. I soon discovered that one of the contractors who supplied us with local produce for the troops left him a bottle of brandy each morning, which he would secrete in a drawer of his desk. He would consume the brandy by the tumblerful and would finish most of the bottle by midday, when his car would call to take us to the mess for lunch. He used to go straight to the bar; I never knew him to come into the dining hall for a meal.

I spent quite a lot of time out of the depot, ensuring that the supplies were being handled and accounted for properly; much in the same way as in the depots in England, but in a more responsible role, as I had frequently to deal with visiting officers. I also made frequent inspections of the petrol sub-depot, located inside the compound.

One day I called to see the major and as I entered his office, the telephone rang. It was the Headquarters office, summoning him to see the colonel. Unfortunately, the major was more than a little intoxicated and I heard later from the adjutant that he had made rather a fool of himself in front of the colonel. Some time later he was reduced to the rank of captain. I felt terribly sorry for him, but I suppose the colonel didn't have much choice. It was the colonel who had told me, in confidence, of the major's experiences and had asked me to keep an eye on him. I had become friendly with the colonel and played squash with him quite regularly at the Peshawar Club.

The major continued in command at the depot for a while and was then replaced by another officer of the same rank. Not long after he left, I heard that he was in the military hospital with hepatitis. I went to see him. He looked very ill, but as soon as I had greeted him, he produced a bottle of brandy from under his pillow and offered me a drink.

A month or so later I was made second in command of the petrol sub-depot.

The officer in charge was Lt Tom Jenkins, who was well known in musical circles in England prior to the war. He had been the leading violinist with the Bournemouth Light Orchestra and had frequently broadcast on the BBC. He was a very likeable character and we got on well together. His strong addiction to cigarette smoking sometimes got him into trouble. Of course, the last place to smoke was inside a petrol depot and he was caught on more than one occasion by the major with a cigarette in his mouth. The new commanding officer was more active than his predecessor and often paid us visits.

Although most of the fuel was in underground tanks, there was still a large quantity held in cans and barrels for the depot vehicles and spillage was inevitable. Altogether, there was something like a quarter of a million gallons of vehicle and aircraft fuel stored there at any given time.

Tom kept a dog, an Alsatian, which he often brought to the depot; it was gentle and affectionate. He asked me to keep an eye on it while he was on vacation, which I did to the best of my ability, considering that I spent most of the day at the depot. His servant was supposed to be looking after the dog, but to my surprise, it turned up one day at the depot on it's own, having found it's way some three miles from Tom's bungalow. There was something strange about its demeanour and when I made to stroke it, it took my wrist in its mouth and sunk its teeth in; it then scampered off.

I was late getting back to the mess that evening and when I arrived one of the chaps asked if I had heard about Tom's dog. It had got out and mingled with the rabid dogs which gather at the refuse dumps and around dustbins, scavenging for food. Ten rupees bounty was paid for every one of these poor creatures that was killed.

Tom's Alsatian had caught rabies from them and early that evening had entered the mess of the Rajputana Rifles Regiment just as they had sat down for dinner. About two hundred officers had chased the dog around the cantonment trying to capture it. It was eventually caught and shot.

I felt somehow responsible and knew that I would have to break the sad news to Tom when he got back.

I considered it wise to report to the medical officer the next morning; he reprimanded me for not calling sooner. He was worried about the fang marks on my wrist. He gave me an injection in my buttock and told me that I would have to have one every day for a fortnight and I was to report to him immediately if I should start feeling unwell.

It would seem that rabies is a ghastly disease to catch. As, far as I am aware, there is still no known cure. The medical officer told me that all the officers who had chased the dog had to be inoculated, as rabies can be caught by absorption; they were in danger, even if they had only come into contact with the dog's saliva.

I was quite friendly with the medical officer, so on about the fourth day of calling for my injection (I had it on alternate sides as the needle must have gone in about two inches) I barged unceremoniously into his surgery, only to find the colonel who commanded the Rajputanas crouched down with his bare, pink bottom pointed in my direction; the medical officer stood by, with the hypodermic needle poised. The colonel turned his head as he heard me burst into the room and glared at me furiously. I beat a hasty retreat.

Tom took the news about his dog very well on his return and although very sad, he did not blame me for what had happened. Almost as soon as he had arrived back he was posted to Army headquarters in Delhi, the reason being, he thought, that he would be readily available to broadcast from the radio station located near the headquarters.

I was put in charge of the petrol depot, which was gratifying, although I was very sorry to see Tom leave. We agreed to make contact again after the war, but sadly he died from cancer soon after returning to England.

The petrol came by rail in tank wagons from Karachi, which is situated on the coast a long way from Peshawar. By the time they arrived at the depot after being in transit for several days they were extremely hot from the rays of the sun.

The engines of the trains being coal-fired, the wagons were backed towards the depot and while still some distance off, were uncoupled and the engines pulled away, leaving the wagons to be manhandled through the gates of the depot and alongside the underground tanks to which they had been allocated; they were then coupled by hose to the inlet valves.

Before decanting could be started, it was my responsibility to check the volume of the fuel in the wagons against the quantities stated in the accompanying documents. This was done by mounting the wagon, removing the seal from the inlet and inserting a calibrated dipstick. I wore gloves for this operation, as the iron rungs of the ladder attached to the wagon were intensely hot.

Invariably there was a greater quantity of fuel than stated in the documents, due to heat expansion. There was a formula to equalise the two figures, using the stated temperature at the time of filling in Karachi and the temperature on arrival. This latter temperature was often over ninety degrees Fahrenheit, in the summer months.

The hatch cover was removed to allow air in for the decanting; the fumes that arose from inside the wagon were heavy and pungent. Masks were worn at this time.

The climate on the North West Frontier varied from being extremely cold in the winter, with snow on the surrounding hills, to scorching heat in the summer.

When the wagon was emptied, the quantity of fuel was checked again by lowering the dipstick into the storage tank.

There were, of course, very strict fire precautions and there was an armed guard at the entrance to the depot, whose instructions were to check every individual entering, regardless of rank, to ensure that they did not carry matches or a cigarette lighter and, if they did, to confiscate the articles and return them when the individual departed. Also and this caused a great deal of trouble, they had to inspect the visitor's footwear and if they had metal studs on their boots, they were obliged to take them off and wear slippers, a supply of which was kept available in the gatehouse storeroom.

Even a tiny spark from a boot stud could have been enough to start a conflagration, should some petrol have been spilled from a can and one can only imagine what could have resulted, given the vast amount of fuel in the depot.

Once a week we carried out fire drill. Mack Sennet always came to mind when I witnessed it. Somehow, the sepoys never mastered the art of running out the fire hose without tripping over it and getting it tangled. The resulting confusion was quite hilarious. I always thanked my lucky stars that we never had a real fire.

News reached me of the impending inspection visit by a very senior officer from Army headquarters in Delhi; it was supposed to be a surprise visit, but these things always leaked out. I decided that the depot needed to be brightened up and I thought it would be a good idea to have the multitude of pipes painted the colour of the fuel they carried – red for motor vehicle fuel, light blue for ninety octane and light green for the hundred octane aircraft fuel. We supplied both the Army and the Air Force.

I got the sepoys to work and they enjoyed themselves splashing paint everywhere. When finished, it was like the setting for a musical comedy. I did wonder afterwards what the visiting general's reaction would have been when he entered the depot, faced by this blaze of colour, but in the event I need not have worried.

There was only the one, very large, entrance to the depot – large enough to allow access by all kinds of vehicles, which they would enter, collect their fuel, make a circuit of the road inside the perimeter wall and exit through the same gateway.

The railway track was buried in the road and so it did not cause any difficulties.

I had checked the length of the road and found it to be almost exactly a quarter of a mile, which brought back to me the days when I used to go training on the track near my home.

Why not, I thought, have a sports day? So we did. I had called a meeting of all the men one evening and put the idea to them. There were no recreational facilities and they were delighted with the idea of racing each other around the circuitous road.

We had relay races, sprint races and longer races, in which I took part. Those of the .men who did not have suitable footwear were loaned slippers from the pile we kept in readiness at the gate. It was a Sunday, when there was little demand for fuel, although we could break off from the racing to supply the occasional visitor. It was unlikely that the general would choose Sunday for his visit.

The men all joined in with enthusiasm; I don't think any of them had had so much fun in years.

An ever-present fire hazard was the long grass inside the depot, which became very dry when the sun was hot, just waiting for something to set it alight, so we used to hire a gang of tribesmen, possibly the same chaps who had besieged the depot, to come every two or three weeks to scythe down the grass. They were made to leave their rifles outside the depot gates, which they collected on their departure. They may have conspired to take over the depot and I don't think we could have handled them

King cobras abounded in the long grass, but the Pathans regarded them with contempt and killed them with their scythes.

For all their roguish manner, you could not help liking the tribesmen, with their flowing garb and colourful turbans, however scruffy, wound carelessly around their heads. They were, for the most part very tall; all wore beards and had an impish cockney-like sense of humour.

The day arrived for the general's visit. I warned all the men and I waited in my office, some way inside the depot, for news of the coming of the *Bara Sahib*. I could see the entrance gate from the office window and I was watching the guards, interested to find out whether they would check the general and his retinue for matches and so on. They had been given strict instructions to do so, but I realised that they could be intimidated by the appearance of very senior officers, with their stars and red epaulettes.

Suddenly, I saw one of the guards turn and come running towards the office; he was very excited on arrival. He had insisted on seeing the soles of the general's boots and when he saw that they had studs, refused to let him enter the depot.

'Well done,' I thought to myself.

I hastily made for the entrance and introduced myself to the general. I told him that, of course, he could enter the depot, provided he changed his boots for the slippers offered to him. He hesitated, no doubt thinking that it would be undignified for him to comply with my request.

He put his head inside, rather dazedly it seemed, to view the colourful scene and appeared somewhat at a loss for words. Then he drew himself to attention, mumbled something like "everything seems to be in order" saluted and turned away. The next moment, the whole cavalcade of staff cars turned and were on their way back to the cantonment.

I don't know how the news of the outcome of the visit got around, but when I returned to the mess in the evening I was greeted with backslapping and crude jokes about intimidating generals. I pointed out to them that it was the office of this same general who had issued the strict fire precaution instructions. I heard little more of the incident, but I did receive a few rather amused glances from some of the senior officers, who messed separately.

The brigade adjutant, a captain, a very smart, dapper figure, with an enormous walrus moustache, more in keeping with the RAF, I used to think – he was constantly stroking it – saw me outside the mess soon after. We had passed the usual courtesy remarks on the few occasions we had met. He said that the general had spoken to the brigadier of his brief visit to the petrol depot and he had told him that he considered that I had acted properly in not allowing him access and was impressed by my refusal to be intimidated by his rank.

He realised that there was an ever-present danger of fire and that the stringent regulations had to be adhered to by everybody.

Major Phelan – it was he who had come down from London to sort out the cooking arrangements at Parkhurst – stood in the doorway of the mess when I returned one evening. He had taken in Peshawar on his tour of India to check on catering arrangements for officers in hotels when they went on vacation.

I noted at the time that his red lapel flashes were very similar to ours of the North West Frontier. We recognized each other immediately and shook hands. He told me that my initiative in informing the War Office of the appalling conditions at the barracks, although strictly out of order, had impressed the hierarchy and had probably contributed to my being recommended for a commission.

His manner, however, was rather condescending, I suppose because of my lowly rank. I had discovered that officers of humble origins and this certainly applied to the major, tended to behave in a more superior manner. He stayed only for a few days and I learnt from Raschid, who had heard it from the major's bearer, that the major suffered from piles and this no doubt had an effect on his demeanour.

I saw him going off one morning in a truck, to inspect something or other and instead of sitting beside the Indian driver, which one would have expected of an officer, he was standing in the back of the truck His affliction in the very hot weather must have been very painful.

VII: The Brigadier's Daughter

The brigadier's daughter was a lovely creature, tall and slim with a heavenly figure and long brown hair hanging loosely over her shoulders.

I had seen her often, swimming in the Peshawar Club pool, but had not approached her, as she had seemed rather aloof and the long period away from women had made me rather shy.

Soon after I was promoted to captain and made second in command of the base supply depot, I was invited by Colonel Shepherd to join him and the brigadier, with their wives, for tea at the club. Tea was traditionally taken on the grass at the side of the bathing pool.

I duly arrived and was surprised and secretly delighted to find that Daphne, the daughter, was also present. We looked across the table into each other's eyes and I was absolutely captivated.

Nothing of military importance was discussed, except for the war in Europe, which we had just heard, had drawn to a successful conclusion for the Allies. Of course, the war with Japan was still continuing.

The colonel told me that there was to be a court of enquiry, as one of our trucks had accidentally hit a buffalo and killed it and it was rather complicated because the owners had claimed that the animal was pregnant and considered that they should receive double the usual compensation. He asked me if I would mind conducting the enquiry.

I said that I would be pleased to do so, although inwardly I was a little concerned as, although my Urdu had progressed quite well, I still had some difficulty in understanding the natives, who spoke quickly and not very clearly.

It was just then, as I had taken a bite from an iced cake and removed it from my mouth, that a giant kite hawk swooped down and took the cake from my fingers. This caused Daphne to shriek with mirth, which drew me further to her. She mentioned her pleasure in swimming up and down the pool and she told me that they were going to have pipes put around which would spray water on it to cool it down. I told her that I usually had a swim after a game of squash and a shower and I found the exercise did me a lot of good.

I was foolish not to ask her whether she also played squash and, if so, if she would like a game with me sometime. I could have kicked myself afterwards, for having lost the opportunity to meet her again.

The court of enquiry was not the ordeal I had expected, mainly because I was ably assisted by a subedar, the equivalent of a sergeant, who could speak perfect English and was able to help me over the difficult linguistic patches. In truth, I was glad to have the chance to meet some of the non-military inhabitants of the town.

The instances when Indian Army officers have behaved badly in the past are legend, but my experiences with my fellow officers, brief though they may have been, had shown me that their philosophy was to treat the natives with kindness and consideration and, above all, to do nothing to demean them, their dignity being of paramount importance to them. There were, in fact, so many of them, sadly, who had little else. I took great pains to conduct the enquiry in a friendly and considerate manner and agreed to the demands, even though they were on the extravagant side, having in mind that the buffalo to them was all that they had had with which to earn a living.

We parted as the best of friends and I promised that the money would be forthcoming without delay.

One of my regular duties was to conduct pay day for all the troops in the army complex. It came around once a month. I always thought that it was a great mistake not to pay the soldiers weekly, although I realized that it would have made a lot more work. Many of the sepoys ran out of money long before the next pay day was due and as a result they got into the hands of moneylenders, who would be waiting around the corner to grab their money as soon as they were paid.

I discovered this when one of the sepoys was posted to another location and he came to ask me if he could have an advance of pay as he was penniless (rupee-less).

When I expressed surprise, as he had been paid only the day previous, he told me about the moneylenders, who took the whole of his pay immediately he had received it and as a result, he was constantly in debt.

I had to make a monthly journey to the Bank of India, situated in the city, to collect the pay money and I always felt a certain amount of trepidation as the teller counted out the thousands of rupee notes, under the gaze of the native customers, clearly lusting after the money. I did not have a guard, only the truck driver, whose strict instructions were to keep the engine running so that we could make a quick getaway.

On one of the trips to the bank, going through the crowded city, my driver accidentally struck a young girl, who fell to the ground. With great presence of mind, the driver stopped the truck and immediately descended, picking up the girl in his arms and depositing her gently in the back of the truck on some sacking.

By the time he had returned to his seat and restarted the engine, a menacing crowd was assembling. We slowly moved through the gesticulating natives, then gathered speed and made for the hospital, which, fortunately, was nearby.

The driver lifted the child from the back of the truck and we entered through the only door of the hospital. By this time a screaming mob was approaching and I hastily closed and bolted the door.

A doctor promptly examined the girl and he told me that she had suffered only minor bruising to a shoulder and one of her legs. He asked me to unbolt the door and open it and lifted up the child and, holding her in his arms, showed her to the crowd and assured them that she was not seriously hurt. He lowered her to the ground and she ran off, no doubt to rejoin her parents.

While this was going on the driver and I had stayed discreetly in the background. The doctor advised us to stay where we were until the crowd had dispersed. He said that we were fortunate that we had made it to the hospital before they had reached us. He had known of a similar incident where the driver of a vehicle, who had knocked down a pedestrian, had been lynched.

This brought home to me the fact that the native population still had a long way to go on the road to becoming civilised. I was to be reminded of this incident at a later date when I visited Calcutta.

Pay day was a long and complicated affair. Many of the sepoys were unable to write their names and so they gave a thumb-print, which was initialled by the havildar, who assisted me in making payment to the several hundred troops.

It was some time later, when checking the records, that it came to light that the havildar had added some non-existing sepoys to the pay list and was pocketing the money.

The havildar was a very pleasant character, as most of them were and I was in some doubt as to the best course of action to take. I decided to consult my commanding officer, who was of the opinion that he should be reprimanded, which surprised me greatly. In the British Army it would certainly have meant a court martial. However, this was the Indian Army, with regulations all of its own. I felt obliged to go along with the major's decision, although I ensured that the havildar was taken off the pay staff and was made to refund the stolen money by means of monthly deductions from his pay.

On another occasion I was approached by a sepoy with tears in his eyes who told me that the subedar in charge of the orderly room had refused him permission to go on compassionate leave to attend the funeral of his mother. I thought this to be heartless of the subedar and told the sepoy that he could leave immediately for his village, which was about two day's journey, way up in the mountains.

When I came across the subedar later in the day I reproached him for his lack of compassion. He confirmed that the sepoy's mother had indeed died ... but some two years earlier. The military police were instructed to bring the sepoy back; he was apprehended half way on his journey.

The next morning the sepoy was brought before me to explain his conduct. He looked me straight in the eye, without a glimmer of remorse. He said that he knew I had not been there very long and thought that he would take advantage of my ignorance of the sepoys' history to try to get leave (*chutti*, in Urdu) but it had not paid off.

Again the major dissuaded me from taking punitive action, saying that they were like naughty children and we must treat them accordingly.

I recalled our briefing before we left the academy on the difficulties we would face when training raw recruits, when, as I was taking a parade of newcomers, I saw that one of the sepoys had his boots on the wrong feet, which must have caused him some discomfort. I gathered afterwards from the havildar, who was the instructor, that none of them had worn footwear before enlisting.

When they were having drill instruction, they were constantly bumping into each other and tripping over. They had great difficulty in keeping in step. It was not easy to keep a smile from one's face.

Weapon training was another comical display, but they really tried hard to master the handling of their rifles. It was some time before they were allowed to practice loading with live ammunition, as there could have been some very unpleasant accidents.

I used often to think of Hilda and the times we had had together on the Isle of Wight, which now seemed a long, long time ago. I recalled an occasion when I had arrived early at Gurnard to meet her.

I decided to have a swim while awaiting her arrival; it was sunny and warm, the sea calm, the sky blue and clear and I swam out a long way and turned over to float on my back. Suddenly I saw an aircraft very high in the sky. It looked the size of a fly.

As I watched, a puff of smoke emerged from the tail and then I heard the thud of heavy gunfire. The plane burst into flames and as I watched, it slowly began to descend in a spiral, disappearing eventually behind a small wood at the rear of the beach; then I heard the explosion and a column of smoke arose, forming a dark backcloth to the trees.

Sometime later I was told that the heavy anti-aircraft battery a couple of miles north of Gurnard had hit the enemy aircraft with a single round; a complete fluke.

Emerging from the sea, dripping wet, I saw Hilda approaching. I went to meet her and impulsively grabbed her and lifted her off her feet. She screamed and beat me with her fists, but I insisted in carrying her to the promenade.

Happy days…

Notwithstanding the inconclusive situation with regard to her fiancé, I had been corresponding with her. She now told me that she had finally given him up and would await my return, however long the war lasted.

This correspondence, which had become more and more passionate, was a source of great comfort to me, being so far from home, I looked forward to her letters each week. I heard only very occasionally from my mother.

Then the letters stopped coming and for several weeks I lay awake at night, wondering what had happened to cause her to stop writing; perhaps she had been killed or injured in an air raid. I continued to write to her, my letters showing increasing concern about her welfare.

Then a letter arrived one day. It was addressed in her handwriting. I hardly dare open it. The news was that she had been obliged to abandon the pianoforte lessons she had been giving, to work in a factory making aircraft components and she had made friends with the foreman and had succumbed to his advances. A baby was expected in about six months.

I went through agonies, mostly of intense sadness, but sometimes with bitterness. I suppose it was understandable for a young woman, in the pressures and uncertainties of war, to let herself go, but at the time I felt betrayed.

Even so, I made enquiries as to the possibility of marrying her by proxy, but I was strongly advised against it by the officer who dealt with personal problems.

Eventually she decided to marry the prospective father and as time went by the hurt I felt slowly began to fade.

It was also because of this involvement with Hilda that I had kept my distance from Daphne. She was in the pool again one evening, all on her own. I had been playing squash with the colonel and thought that I would have a dip before I went to the mess for dinner. I dived off the springboard and made a perfect entry into the water, causing hardly a splash. As I surfaced, I came up quite near Daphne, who was clapping her hands in appreciation of my well-executed dive.

I swam towards her and in a moment we were in a passionate embrace. We agreed to meet secretly after dinner and go for a walk. I met her behind the squash courts and we began our stroll with our arms around each other's waist.

It was a warm, balmy evening and we could smell the evening jasmine wafting in the warm air – altogether charming and at the same time exciting. We came to a deep gully which took the rain away when it fell heavily and dramatically for a brief period in the winter.

She guided me down the gully and through a copse of wild mango trees, at the centre of which was a thick matting of grass. She lay on the grass and gently pulled me down beside her, ignoring the strong possibility of snakes and scorpions. The skirt of her thin floral dress was up beyond her knees. She had no stockings on. She turned and put her arms around me. Her perfume was overpowering.

She pulled down one of the straps of her dress and a small breast, surmounted by a pink nipple, nestling in a tiny brown circle, sprung forth. I leaned forward to take the nipple between my lips, massaging it with my tongue. She sighed and my right hand found a knee and travelled up her thigh. I realised then, that she had on only the dress. She turned onto her back and pulled me towards her. Both my hands travelled up inside her dress until they reached her armpits. Then they were holding her breasts and the thumbs caressed her nipples.

She sat up and took off her dress and lay down again, quite naked. I soon divested myself of my light jacket and other clothing and we closely embraced.

We made love for at least half an hour. It was the first time for me and I wanted to make it last as long as possible. Finally, we fell asleep. I had never known before the wonderful, relaxed feeling that comes after love making, that goes right down and causes your feet to tingle.

We were still closely embraced when we awoke to the noise of the crickets. I was about to get dressed, but she insisted on further lovemaking. I was surprised to find that I had no difficulty in obliging her. I had always thought that it took some time to recover.

We had another glorious, twenty minutes or so and then got dressed and made out way back to the rear of the club, where we kissed and promised to meet again the following evening.

However, Daphne did not appear the next day, or the day after, which was very disappointing and I wondered what the reason was for her non-appearance.

I was summoned to see the colonel, who told me that the officer in charge of a small depot at Risalpur had been taken ill and it was essential that I proceeded there immediately to take over.

I left the next morning by jeep, still wondering why Daphne hadn't turned up.

Risalpur was about a hundred miles away, in the desert and reputed to be one of the hottest spots in the country. The office, when I entered it, was stiflingly hot; there was not, of course, any air conditioning and the one small fan merely succeeded in moving the hot air around. Over the windows, outside, were raffia blinds, known as *tas tas khatis*, which were hosed down periodically by the *chowkidar*, the evaporating water helping to cool the place down.

Scorpions abounded. Emerging from the bathroom the next morning, with just a towel around me and wearing slippers, I was confronted by an enormous, almost transparent scorpion, its poison plainly visible in its tail, which curled upwards from its body.

There was nothing handy with which to ward it off, but I saw a bottle of glue on the table, which I had been using the previous evening and I grabbed it and poured the contents of the bottle over the creature. I found a shovel in the kitchen and managed to pick the scorpion up and deposit it outside.

Later, I went out to wash it clean with the water hose and it scuttled away. My philosophy has always been never to kill any creature, even those that may menace life and health. Some time earlier I had been stung on a toe by a scorpion, which had got into the bed, but apart from some swelling I did not suffer much discomfort. Scorpion stings can, however, be very dangerous and I heard stories of people being seriously ill after an attack.

My hair was beginning to thin and I was somewhat worried that I was going to be prematurely bald, so I decided it would be a good opportunity, being the only officer in the depot, to cut my hair really short; I had heard that it promoted stronger growth. I got rather carried, away and in fact I removed almost every sign of hair, thinking that, in the heat, it would soon grow back.

I had been at the depot only a few days when I received a message to report back to Peshawar.

I felt rather embarrassed to appear again before the colonel, virtually hairless, to be told that he had had second thoughts about my temporary transfer and had decided, after all, that I was performing a more useful function in Peshawar and that someone else would be taking over in Risalpur.

Daphne, I learned later, had gone away to Simla, in the hills, with her mother, to escape the heat. I, of course, believed this, though very despondent at the thought that I would very likely not be seeing her again.

It was not until some time later that I heard our little escapade had been witnessed by one of the bearers and of course had spread like wildfire among his fellow workers and inevitably reached the ears of an officer and ultimately the brigadier, Daphne's father.

The brigadier was a close friend of my colonel, both being regular army officers and it became evident that my posting to Risalpur was to get me "out of the clutches of the brig's daughter" as one of my fellow junior officers had put it. My recall to Peshawar was after the departure of Daphne to Simla.

It would seem that for all her sweetness and apparent inno-cence she was something of a man-eater and had frequently been sent away, out of reach of one (or more) of the officers. Not that I was complaining at having been one of her 'victims' – more truthfully sad at the termination of our brief relation-ship; a delightful, memorable experience, which I enjoyed in retrospect.

I had suffered a very long gruelling day, some weeks later and had decided to go to bed early. I was just settling down with a novel, wearing nothing and with just a sheet over me, mosqui-toes buzzing around the net, which enveloped the bed, when I heard a tap at the window. I ignored it, thinking that it was just something that had blown against the pane. Then it was repeated. I moved the mosquito net to one side, got out of bed and stood naked, opening the window to find out what was making the noise.

The warm, scented air blew against me. I could not believe my eyes. By the light of the moon, I could just make out that it was Daphne! She clambered through the window and we grasped each other in a passionate embrace. She told me, breathlessly, that her mother had been obliged to return to Peshawar to see her husband on a legal matter concerning their property in England and she had insisted on Daphne coming with her. She would, no doubt, have worried what Daphne might get up to if left alone, I thought to myself.

Daphne said that she knew where my bungalow was and had told her parents that she was going for a walk to get some air before retiring for the night.

We were soon in bed together, making up for lost time, being reasonably confident that on this occasion we were not being observed.

It was another fantastic experience, but all too short. She had to leave and we kissed passionately in the moonlight, by the window, before I helped her out. She had told me that they would be in Peshawar a few days and, if possible, she would make me another visit before they left again for Simla.

I had been feeling rather guilty since, after the last episode, the colonel had spoken to me briefly on the subject of Daphne. He had been very decent about it and we had continued to play squash together. He said that he appreciated how difficult it was for a young man, away from home, to resist the advances, of a young, nubile woman, intent on sexual satisfaction. He added that the brigadier and his wife found Daphne a bit of a problem. They had brought her from England to escape the bombing, but now the war in Europe was over, they were considering sending her back to take up her studies, which had been neglected. She was only nineteen, he said, and the brigadier thought it too early for her to consider marriage.

I was not actually told to stay away from Daphne, but the suggestion had been made – not that it appeared to be any sort of problem, as she was then safely away in Simla. But what sort of young man could spurn a beautiful young woman who turns up at night more-or-less demanding to be made love to? How could I have resisted?

I felt a bit of a devil next morning when I visited the mess for breakfast. Not all the chaps did this; they found that *chota hazri*, consisting of a cup of tea and biscuits, usually taken in bed, was sufficient for them.

My fellow officers were discussing Daphne, which was strictly against army etiquette. There is a rule in army circles that women are never the subject of conversation in the mess. However, as I entered, all eyes were turned on me. They asked me whether I had heard the news of Daphne's return. Of course I lied and said I had not.

"You had better look out for yourself," one of them said, jokingly. "She'll have you in the copse again if you are not very careful!"

"You should be so lucky, " said another.

I knew that if I had told them what had occurred the previous evening they would have subjected me to continuous ribald banter and I would have felt that I had betrayed Daphne.

I went about my business at the base depot. We had another intake of raw recruits and I was becoming accustomed to their naivety. They were invariably a nice bunch of chaps, very eager to learn. We had started English classes for them in the evening and they were always enthusiastic. Although the classes were voluntary, I cannot ever remember any of them not attending.

I was glad that the officer in charge had not brought up earlier the subject of my affair with Daphne, although it seemed to be common knowledge. He was a married man and no doubt had other matters, apart from running the depot, of more concern to him.

Early in the evening of the next day I was out for a stroll along the Mall, on my own, just after dinner, when whom should I see, coming towards me, but Daphne. I felt a sudden rush of blood to my face on seeing her again so soon and in daylight. She looked radiant and I felt a strong desire to take her in my arms then and there. But on meeting I merely wished her good evening and said what a lovely evening it was, which was trite, as it was nearly always a lovely evening, but what an exceptionally lovely evening, seeing this beautiful girl again, her eyes shining, her lips pouting.

She asked me how I was and I said, "fine" and then, in a lowered voice, "all the better for seeing you last night…"

I asked her whether it had been decided when they would be returning to Simla and she told me that Mummy hadn't made up her mind, but that it certainly would not be for a few days. She then asked me if we could meet again one evening, perhaps that night, as her parents would be playing bridge; how about the copse again?

"Not a good idea," I said. Clearly she had not heard that we were observed on the last occasion. What about the squash courts? I had a key to the courts and to the dressing rooms. I could book a court for the last session at eight o'clock, by which time everybody would have gone.

"Sounds a good idea," she said. "See you there at eight. Don't forget to bring some *doo dahs*."

So... I was about to be one of her victims again! What a pleasant thought. I wondered what she meant by 'doo dahs' and then it suddenly came to me that she meant condoms. I had heard they were available in the market.

I realized that I would have to be careful. If she became pregnant, the brigadier would not be very amused; it would inevitably prejudice any chance of my further promotion.

I arrived at the courts well before eight o'clock and as, presumably, we would not be playing squash, having better things to do, I decided to take a shower. Everybody had left and I had just soaped myself down when I heard the door of the washroom open and the next moment Daphne was standing before me, dressed in a white short-sleeved shirt and white shorts.

She decided to strip off and join me under the shower and we soaped each other all over and massaged each other, then rubbed our bodies together. Daphne started to become very passionate but I stopped her from going too far; I didn't want there to be an abrupt halt to our lovemaking.

The games room was just along the passage, where there was a massage table, so we hurriedly towelled ourselves down and made for the door. On entering the passage the cleaner appeared, complete with bucket and mop. I had forgotten about him. He was a small chap, with a wizened face and he was perpetually smiling. As he turned from closing the door of a cubicle, he looked at us in some amazement, his grin becoming even wider than usual. He gazed, firstly at Daphne, completely naked, and then at me.

He told me that he was just going to leave and I said that I had keys and would lock up after we left. I was somewhat concerned that he would tell his friends about us and I added that if he promised to say nothing of our meeting, to anyone, I would give him ten rupees the next time I saw him. He smilingly agreed.

He could not take his eyes off Daphne. It was probably the first time he had seen a naked white woman.

Daphne led me to the games room and lay down on the table. I asked her if she would like me to massage her and she agreed. I knew where the bearer kept the oils. Unfortunately, I was careless in opening the bottle and the oil cascaded over Daphne's breasts and ran downwards. I tried to arrest the flow and in doing so unwittingly grabbed her most intimate parts. Far from being offended, she asked me to do it again. She squealed with delight.

'What a girl!' I thought.

By now I was trembling with anticipation and couldn't wait to get on the table with Daphne. We were soon rubbing our bodies together, the oil adding to the enjoyment. Just as our lovemaking came to an end, I suddenly remembered the 'doo dahs'.

'What a fool!' I thought. I didn't suppose Daphne had taken any precautions. I asked her, as casually as I was able, whether she had.

"No," she responded. "There's nowhere I know of to get anything." She also realized that I had been forgetful.

She wanted a repeat performance, this time using the doo-dahs, but I wasn't able to oblige; a problem we men have to face sometimes.

We returned to the washroom for another shower before getting dressed. We were silent; no doubt both thinking of the possible consequences of our affair.

I couldn't help thinking that if she had never used contraceptives and if it was true that she had had a number of lovers, why hadn't she become pregnant before? Perhaps I was the first to be careless about the doo-dahs. And why didn't the subject arise on the first occasion of our lovemaking? I must confess that I had been rather naïve. Perhaps I was worrying unnecessarily.

I didn't see Daphne again before she returned with her mother to Simla a few days later. I still wondered whether there would be any consequences from our affair, but as time passed and I heard nothing, I assumed that all was well.

The cleaner at the club kept his word and no news of my further liaison with Daphne ever leaked out. He did attempt to obtain more money from me, but I told him that if he continued I would make sure he was dismissed. I had no intention of allowing him to blackmail me.

And so ended *l'affaire Daphne*... or so I thought.

VIII: *Fun With Friends*

David, a friend, commanded a detachment of the Camel Corps; he was a major. For a time we were obliged to share one of the bungalows, as they were all being refurbished. They had very large entrances and spacious rooms, with high ceilings to enable the heat to rise. The floors were of stone.

On one occasion, I had returned early from the depot and I was sitting in the lounge, cooling off under the ceiling fan, when David appeared on his horse, a beautiful grey Arab stallion. He came through the entrance, still mounted and stopped short of the table at which I was seated. The horse threw up its head and neighed and I gave it one of the biscuits I had been munching.

David was great fun and I enjoyed my short stay with him. He, too, had some classical records, which we used to listen to together.

In the mornings, his groom would bring the horse from the stables and leave it, untethered, in the front garden; David would go outside and whistle and the horse would trot over to him.

David was frequently out on manoeuvres with the camels and we always knew when they were returning, because of the smell, which wafted several miles ahead of them. They were not very lovable creatures; during the mating season they were muzzled, as they would bite and they were not particular about which part of your anatomy they attacked. There was more than one eunuch wandering the byways of Peshawar.

Sometimes when on manoeuvre, David told me, they would have an elephant, with a mahout[1] bringing up in the rear of the procession. Quite what the function of the elephant was, or indeed that of the camels, in modern warfare, I never could understand. Very charming, but totally useless, of course.

On one occasion, David discovered on returning that the elephant had disappeared. Not an easy object to lose, one would have thought, but David found it very difficult to ride shotgun, with the multitude of camels to look after.

It appeared that the mahout had sold the elephant to some-body as they had passed through a village. It transpired that he received only a thousand rupees for the animal; not very much for about three tons of elephant.

The mahout initially denied that he had sold the animal, but the truth eventually emerged. He was ordered to get the elephant back, under pain of severe punishment if he failed.

I said to David that the war would have to be suspended in the meantime. I'm afraid my sense of humour wasn't always appreciated!

There were a number of Arab horses and I sometimes went for a trot on one of them. Not being a very good horseman, I kept to the compound. One day my horse took it into its head to try to jump the surrounding wall, about five feet high. Just

---

[1] Elephant driver.

as it approached the wall at the gallop, it changed its mind, swerved away and shot me out of the saddle. To the amazement of everybody, including myself, I landed on both feet, with my knees bent and stood upright without falling over. I took a bow, much to the amusement of the onlookers.

We had to take turns to supervise the catering and to do the accounts – a chore I did not much enjoy, as my fellow officers were always complaining, either about the quality of the food, or about the size of their mess bills. Latterly, when I tired of their complaints, I took to eating my meals alone in a small annexe attached to the dining room.

The only Irishman in the mess, another Paddy, refused ever to eat curry and as this was more or less our staple diet, making special provision for him was a daily problem.

It seemed to me that it didn't matter much what food I provided as, whatever it was, he always insisted in smothering it with tomato sauce, which wasn't easy to acquire and was very expensive.

One of Paddy's favourite tricks, was to throw raw eggs upwards towards the ceiling, endeavouring to avoid the rotating blades of one of the giant ceiling fans. He was not always successful and the fan would hit the egg and spatter the walls and table; all very amusing, but tiresome when it came to cleaning up the mess.

He was a keen photographer and had some very nice nude female photos, which he had had framed and hung at intervals on the walls, up the staircase leading to the mess room. Everybody admired the photos and they were a source of pride for Paddy, until, one day, they all disappeared. The poor chap went around accusing everybody, but the photos had vanished. Things often went missing, as if spirited away. I have no doubt that one of the Indian servants had taken the photographs. He probably got a good price for them in the market.

Another character was Max, who was always boasting of his conquests with the hospital nurses of the Queen Alexander Military Nursing Service or 'Quamis' for short. He was a small man, heavily bespectacled, who was never promoted above the rank of lieutenant, because of his leftist views, we all thought, which he made no secret of. I never could understand what the nurses saw in him, but perhaps it was just wishful thinking on his part. He had obtained a first class degree at Oxford, where he had made the acquaintance of Pandit Nehru, destined to become India's first prime minister.

Max and I got on quite well. His politics didn't bother me, and so, when the time came for us to take a vacation, we decided to do a tour of India together.

En route to Delhi from Peshawar, the train was running several hours late, due mainly to the time taken for meals. There were no restaurant cars and the train had to stop while we all proceeded to the nearest eating-place. The meals could take some time to prepare, but as none of us was in a hurry, we languished over the proceedings. The engine driver would come to implore us to hurry up, as he would be severely admonished for arriving late in Delhi.

It was a long journey and we were due in Delhi the next morning. Knowing we were running very late, I did not hurry to arise when the day broke, feeling sleepy after several pegs of whisky, but, unknown to me, the train had made up the time during the night and we, in fact, had arrived at Delhi on time.

The train had pulled into the station when I was still asleep in the couchette in my pyjamas and I had to dress in full view of the other passengers who were already disembarking.

Max insisted in calling at the administration buildings in an endeavour to see Pandit Nehru, but when we arrived we found that Nehru was out of town.

We did not stay long in Delhi, as we had a lot of ground to cover in the month we were to be away, however, we found time to visit Old Delhi, travelling by *tonga*.[2] The driver was beating a poor, emaciated donkey with a stick, to urge it up the slopes, but after a while I told Max I could stand it no longer. I instructed the driver to stop, then alighted and grabbed his stick, which I broke in half. We proceeded the rest of the way on foot.

We managed to get inside the grounds of the Lal Quila, the Red Fort, and mingle with the crowds. The fort, of red sand-stone, hence its name, is a truly enormous construction.

The crowds were large, gathered around a variety of perform-ances – natives playing their fiddles to induce snakes into rising from their baskets and, the most spectacular perform-ance, the Indian rope trick. This was something I had heard about but had regarded with scepticism. Now, here in front of our eyes, it was being performed.

---

[2] A donkey-drawn, two-wheeled carriage.

A thick hessian rope began slowly to rise from a large basket, straight up into the air, with no visible signs of support. Being in the open, there could have been no invisible wire pulling it up. It stopped, absolutely erect, at about twenty-five feet.

A small boy, wearing a loincloth and turban, emerged from the basket and slowly ascended the rope, hand over hand, looking straight upwards. As he reached the top he just disappeared.

I suppose it was mass hypnotism, I don't really know. I cannot recall feeling even slightly bemused.

We were ushered on, with no opportunity to question anybody about the performance. I couldn't help wondering what had happened to the boy. Did they have to find another one every time they gave a performance?

After a meal, we made our way to the station, where we were intending to catch a train to Calcutta, our next port of call; a journey of about six hundred miles. Arriving at the station, we found a large crowd of Ghurkhas with their wives and children carrying an assortment of large bundles, cooking utensils hanging outside, which jangled together as the Ghurkhas shoved one another towards the platform entrance.

We obtained our tickets and eventually made our way through the crowd and onto the train. In our compartment was a young lieutenant who told us that he had only recently been commissioned and the first task allotted to him had been to conduct the party of Ghurkhas and their families to Calcutta and then to Kathmandu, where they were to be demobilised.

This being his first assignment, he was anxious to make a good job of it.

When the train stopped at Allahabad for a scheduled twenty minutes, the lieutenant decided to get off to stretch his legs. We warned him that as the train was running late, it might not stop for long. This proved to be the case and the officer was left behind when the train pulled out. Because of my rank, I had no alternative but to seek out the Ghurkhas' senior Viceroy's Commissioned officer, a subedar,[3] to take over command of the contingent. The subedar was highly amused to learn that his commanding officer had missed the train and pointed out that the officer was in possession of all the leave passes and other documentation.

The huge contingent of Ghurkhas emerged onto the platform when we arrived at Howrah station in Calcutta, and Max and I had to fight our way to the exit. We did our best to explain to the ticket collector, who unfortunately spoke neither Urdu nor English (there are many languages in India) why there were no travel passes for the troops, who were by then crowding around us. The subedar arrived and joined us in trying to persuade the railway official to allow the Ghurkhas through, but to no avail.

I told Max and the subedar to stay there while I went in search of the Railway Transport Officer, to get him to sort the matter out. I found the RTO, a captain, in the main terminal building. He had been advised of the movement of the Ghurkhas and said he would take over. He said the troops

---

[3] equivalent in rank to a staff sergeant major.

128

would have to wait until the officer arrived with the passes. There was another train due from Allahabad in a few hours and he was sure to be on it.

Having returned to tell Max, the subedar and the ticket collector that the RTO would be coming to take charge of the troops, Max and I proceeded outside the station in search of a tonga to take us to the Grand Hotel, which had been recommended to us.

We had been travelling in our heavy uniforms, as it was quite cool when we left Peshawar and they were now uncomfortable in the humid heat of Calcutta. We were looking forward to having a shower and changing into more suitable attire.

The Grand Hotel, a sumptuous affair, was located in a main thoroughfare named Chowringhee. As soon as we arrived and registered our names, we were told by the manager that there were riots in the city and we should not venture far from the hotel; also, that the *dhobis*[4] were on strike, as were the refuse collectors. This explained the huge piles of rubbish we had seen on our way from the station. Not much of a welcome to the city we had travelled so far to see.

I was struck by the startling contrast between the luxury of the hotel and all it offered and the pitiful beggars lying on the pavement outside, on rags and old clothing; some of them on boards with what looked like pram-wheels attached. They were the legless ones, I was told, who used their hands to propel themselves along.

---

[4] Washer men.

129

The loss of limbs was attributable to leprosy, which prevailed in the slum districts, although it had been known for some of the desperately poor people to maim themselves deliberately, to invoke pity and hence more *baksheesh*.[5]

Max told me that he had been contributing to a well-known Sunday newspaper and that he was keen to write an article about the riots, so after dinner we emerged from the side door of the hotel into the street and made our way towards the city, the direction having been given us by one of the porters. We had avoided the main entrance, as no one else appeared to be going out, because of the riots, and we did not wish to be conspicuous.

It was not long before we sighted a screaming mob coming towards us with sticks and knives raised and they chased us as we fled. We had changed into light, khaki uniforms and the sight of these seemed to provoke them. We managed to elude the crowd by turning down a dark alleyway, where we cowered as they tore past us along the road.

We continued down the alleyway and eventually emerged into a larger thoroughfare. In the distance we could hear the cries of another mob and then they appeared, torches illuminating their frenzied faces.

From the other end of the road, a jeep appeared, with a huge stars and stripes flag mounted on the front, flapping in the breeze as it passed us. Approaching the mob, it stopped abruptly and two American soldiers got out, no doubt having in mind to try to quell the crowd. They were armed with

[5] Gratuity.

rifles, but before they could take any action, they were seized and their rifles taken from them. They were then clubbed ferociously with the guns and dragged onto the bonnet of the jeep. One of the assailants had obtained a petrol can from the rear of the vehicle and the contents were poured over both the jeep and the prostrate Americans; then everything went up in flames. It all happened in a matter of a few moments. We were too far away to attempt to intervene, not that we would have stood the faintest of chances against the mob. It was a sickening sight to witness and we stood aghast as the crowd of natives milled around the conflagration. We were completely at a loss to understand why they had behaved in this appalling manner.

By this time Max and I were completely lost and it had turned very dark. We found ourselves going down more alleyways, colliding with piles of rubbish and rotting vegetation, dogs scampering in all directions after being disturbed, most of them, no doubt, victims of rabies. The smells were intolerable.

We saw some flickering lights and as we neared them, we could make out lines of huts, squalid, filthy looking constructions, illuminated by oil lamps and fires from which grey smoke emerged and slowly spiralled upwards, disappearing into the dark night. We had arrived in the slum quarter, where the poorest of the inhabitants of Calcutta live and where Mother Teresa did such marvellous work, tending the sick, many with leprosy and comforting the poor mothers and their children.

We decided to explore the area. Perhaps surprisingly, after our experience of only a short time earlier, we did not feel ourselves to be at risk, walking down the badly lit alleyways, although we were constantly accompanied by crowds of children, many of them carrying babies, calling 'Baksheesh sahib'. I gave them all the money I had, which wasn't very much.

I was most impressed by the pleasant demeanour of the people, who greeted us with smiles and words of welcome. Perhaps they just saw us as providers of baksheesh, but I don't really think so.

Some time later we found ourselves outside the station, at which we had arrived earlier in the day. It seemed a long time ago. By now it was quite late, but we managed to find a tonga wallah, who was prepared to take us back to the hotel, for double the usual fee. Fortunately, Max still had some money.

It was our inability the next morning to have our linen washed, because of the dhobi strike, which finally decided us not to prolong our stay in Calcutta. The oppressive heat, the stench in the streets and the riots, had combined to make things unpleasant.

Max had managed to borrow a typewriter from the hotel management and was pounding away with his story about the riots, while I went downstairs to pay the bills.

I could not believe my eyes as I entered the reception hall. There, with her back towards me, not twenty feet away, was Daphne. I recognised her instantly, as she was wearing the rather distinctive dress she had worn on our first rendezvous.

It immediately brought back vivid recollections of the occasion.

She was engrossed in conversation with a lady I took to be her mother, although I could not see her face. I wondered what they were doing in Calcutta, so far from the North West Frontier.

Feeling rather nonplussed, I went to the receptionist to pay the accounts. Just as I turned away, a voice which had been haunting my dreams, together with other things, said "Hello". It was Daphne, at my shoulder.

"What are you doing here?" I asked, trying to keep calm.

"Daddy has been posted to Burma to help in the peace negotiations," she replied, "and we have been seeing him off."

"I suppose you will be returning to Peshawar right away – or are you staying in Simla?" I enquired.

"Neither," she said, "we are spending a few days here with friends and then we are travelling to Bombay to catch a boat back to England."

There was a pause.

"It's very nice to see you again," I said. "I often think of our last meeting."

"So do I," she responded, with a mischievous look in her eyes. "My mother has gone to lie down for a while, the heat is too much or her, a lot more humid than in the North West. What are you doing?"

"I have just been paying our bills, that is my bill and that of Max, my friend. We are on vacation together."

I told her of our experiences the night before.

"Max is busy writing an account of the riots for a newspaper. We are planning to leave this evening for Darjeeling."

Daphne lowered her voice.

"I'm feeling desperate for a gruno," she said. "Must be the heat." She had a strange vocabulary sometimes, probably from her schooldays. I had never met the word "gruno" but I knew what she meant.

"It can't be long," I said. "Max will he wondering what has happened to me."

"Can't you phone him and tell him you have met a friend?" she said. She seemed determined to have her way, so I telephoned Max and told him I had met an acquaintance, which was true and that I was going up to his room for a chat, which wasn't quite true.

"What's your room number?" enquired Daphne.

"Number 134, second floor," I replied. 'See you there in ten minutes.' And she was off.

I bounded up the stairs to my room. Fortunately, Max and I had been obliged to take rooms on different floors, so the chance of meeting him was unlikely.

I decided to have a quick shower, as I was feeling sticky from the heat, the hotel fans not being very effective. Just as I had finished towelling myself down, there was a gentle knock on the door. I went to open it and Daphne quickly slid inside. Seeing me with just the towel around me she said, 'All ready, I see!"

"I was feeling like a shower," I said.

"I think I'll have one myself," she said. "I hope you don't mind…"

"Of course not. You will find a towel in the cabinet."

I lay on the bed, in eager anticipation, the giant ceiling fan overhead wafting a gently breeze over my body. 'What a slice of luck,' I thought.

Daphne entered from the bathroom, not bothering with a towel.

"I'm afraid I haven't any doo-dahs," I said. 'I hadn't planned on meeting you again."

"That's alright," she replied, "I managed to get some in the market."

I looked at her.

"Just in case…" she added, looking a little apologetic.

I shan't go into details about what followed; I will only say that she had clearly been missing her riding lessons and badly needed the exercise.

Before we parted, Daphne gave me her London address and asked me to get in touch with her when I got back to England. I gathered that her family also had a house in the country. It seemed that they were very well off.

I got dressed and went straight to Max's room. He had just finished his article and was reading the Times of India. He read out to me some of the accounts of the riots. I had wondered whether to tell him what had happened, but decided not to do so. I just said that I had met this chap, who had been on a course with me. He didn't pursue the matter, which was a relief. It saved me the embarrassment of having to tell further lies. It doesn't come easy to me to tell untruths.

We had managed to book seats on a train leaving late that evening for Siliguri. It would be necessary to take a further train up to Darjeeling. The journey took most of the night and dawn was breaking as we reached Siliguri.

Breakfast of tea, chapattis[6] with honey and ghee[7] and some local sweetmeats fortified us for the trip up the mountains.

The train to Darjeeling was a ramshackle affair and the gradients were so steep it was necessary for it to shunt backwards and forwards. Sometimes the track went through a village and the train proceeded so slowly passengers were able to jump off to make a purchase from one of the stalls and then jump back on again.

Although Darjeeling is about seven thousand feet above sea level and the Himalayas some fifty miles away, it is necessary to look upwards to see the peaks of Mount Everest and Kanchanjunga. This perhaps conveys something of the awesome majesty of these mountains.

---

[6] unleavened bread.
[7] clarified butter.

We wandered around during the day, visiting shops and places of interest, enjoying the crisp mountain air after the torrid atmosphere of Calcutta.

As the sun set and the shadows from the mountains lengthened, the temperature fell and we were glad to make our way back to the small hotel where we were staying. There was a log fire in the dining room, which warmed us as we ate our dinner of curried lamb and rice.

Soon after breakfast the next morning, we made plans for our departure, back to Siliguri and then on to Shillong, which meant crossing the Brahmaputra river. We decided to make the journey down to Siliguri by coach, instead of taking the slow train, being unaware that the coach drivers in that part of the world were notorious for their reckless behaviour.

The journey was hair-raising, to say the least. How the vehicle kept to the steep twisting roads was a miracle. I would swear that the coach had no brakes. Just as with the trains, many of the passengers clung to the outside. There was vehicle debris adhering to the sides of the ravines. I doubt that the driver used much petrol, just the force of gravity.

We were thankful to arrive back in Siliguri still intact, although the other passengers appeared quite relaxed, no doubt used to the experience.

We estimated that the coach took roughly a quarter of the time to descend than the train had taken going upwards.

It was not long before the next train for Shillong was due to leave and we hurried to the office to get tickets. The journey was exciting, the train crossing a bridge high over the Brahmaputra river, in a deep gorge. The scenery was most spectacular. A short spell in Shillong and we were on our way to Cherapunji, which Max was keen to visit. It is reputed to have the highest rainfall in the world.

The meteorological officer, an Englishman, gave us some interesting information. He told us that on one single day the previous year, the rainfall had been equivalent to that of the average rainfall in England for a whole year.

His equipment was very basic, the main item being a calibrated glass beaker, which he had to go out frequently in the pouring rain to empty. This was of course, during the rainy season, early in the year. The sun shone brightly when we were there.

The officer showed us his records, which were quite astounding. He also drew our attention to the roofs of the dwellings and the shops, all of which were of corrugated iron to withstand the deluge when it came.

We were directed to a small boarding house, where we spent the night. Cherapunji is rather remote and they do not get many visitors.

The next morning we started on our long journey back to Peshawar, our next destination being Benares, on the river Ganges. This is an interesting town, the shops selling a wide variety of brassware, wooden boxes and other articles of wood, all delicately carved with intricate designs. There were also, of course, in many of the shops, beautiful saris, for which Benares is well known.

It was a remarkable experience, to witness the citizens of the town by the riverside, bathing themselves in the holy waters of the Ganges. While bathing, they also took the opportunity to wash their clothing.

Lining the river were the *ghats* – large wooden constructions on which bodies are burned – the ashes being scattered and carried downstream by the river, this having a religious significance.

It would seem, however, that the use of the *ghats* is confined to adults, because as we watched, we saw a sorrowful man, presumably a father, deposit a small infant, wrapped in a shroud, into the river. He waited to witness the tiny bundle moving slowly away, no doubt, in his mind, into the arms of Allah.

We had left to the last, the place which we had looked forward to the most to visit, which was Agra, the home of that most outstanding specimen of architecture, the Taj Mahal, created by the emperor Shah Jahan as a memorial to his most beloved wife, Mumtaz Mahal.

It was in 1631 when construction commenced and it is said to have, taken 20,000 workers 22 years to complete.

There cannot possibly be a more beautiful building on earth. It is a miracle of perfection. One wonders what sort of person designed it. He must have visualised from the outset what it was going to look like, which to me is incredible. Like Brahms composing a whole symphony in his mind before committing it to paper.

When we arrived at our hotel, our welcome by the proprietor was quite astounding, until we realised that he had mistaken us for Army Headquarters inspectors. I recalled that our uniform insignia was very similar to that worn by Major Phelan, who was, in fact, an inspector from Headquarters.

I was persuaded by Max not to disillusion the proprietor and we spent a very enjoyable time there, being treated like lords. The staff could not do enough for us.

We had intended to stay just a few days in Agra, but eventually we spent a whole week there. Each morning, after breakfast, we would make our way through the market place to visit the temple. It was a feast for the eyes and we could not see it often enough.

On our departure, we were told that there would be no charge for our meals and accommodation. Max was quite happy to accept this, hut although I had gone along, reluctantly, with the pretence of being an inspector, I was not prepared to benefit from the situation by not paying for my stay at the hotel and I insisted on the proprietor presenting me with my bill. Max had no alternative but to do the same, rather to his annoyance. I am usually very easygoing and do not make a fuss over trivialities, but on this occasion I stood firm.

Acceptance of the gesture by the proprietor would have been quite wrong, as he had no doubt made it in an attempt to influence the report on the hotel, which he imagined we would be making.

We had to spend a few hours in Delhi, awaiting our connection to Peshawar and Max took the opportunity to call again to try to see Pandit Nehru, but he was still away. The train taking us to Peshawar stopped for a short spell at Lahore, where I had had my wallet stolen, two years or more earlier.

IX: *Farewell to Peshawar*

On our return, we found that several of the wartime officers had been demobilised and were preparing to return to the United Kingdom; also, a number of Army units had been moved, or were about to be moved, to other locations. The threat of invasion of India by the Russians, through Afghanistan, had largely disappeared.

It was made clear to me the day following my return, that I would continue to have a function for some time as the Army detachments and RAF units remaining in the area would still require to draw supplies and fuel from the depot.

Max soon left on his way back to England, ultimately to become the General Secretary of the National Union of Teachers. We did not meet again.

Just at this time, General Bill Slim, who had commanded the 14th Army in Burma, arrived at Peshawar. He was doing a tour of Army units prior to taking over as Commander in Chief of the Indian Army.

He was a remarkable character, having come through the ranks from private soldier. He was a down to earth, cheerful, no-nonsense individual with a very strong personality.

All the officers remaining were assembled for a lecture and he demonstrated to us on a blackboard how the battles surrounding Kohima and Imphal had been conducted.

The Japanese had penetrated India from Burma, across the river Chindwin and intended to capture both Kohima and Imphal, which would have provided them with springboards for a full-scale invasion of India.

It was vital that we retained these two strategic towns and also possession of the road link between them.

The battles which ensued were horrific, the difficulties in moving through the unfriendly terrain made much worse by the incessant torrential rain.

However, the conditions proved to be a determining factor in the defeat of the Japanese Army. The 14th Army had established airfields and they received a constant supply of supplies and replacement equipment, delivered by the RAF. The Japanese, on the other hand, relied on overland supplies, which were delivered only spasmodically, due to their over extended lines. Heavy rain made the tracks virtually impassable.

In the latter stages of the confrontation, the Japanese were reduced to consuming just water and whatever edible vegetation they could find for their existence.

It was interesting to hear, direct from an Army commander, how he had gone about the task of defeating the enemy. His main consideration and I suppose this goes for all military people in a similar position, was how to achieve the objectives with the minimum number of casualties.

143

He spoke of the options for each attack and gave his reasons for the choice, using a ruler to indicate on a map of the area, just as a schoolmaster would demonstrate the solving of a mathematical problem to his pupils. He was quite dispassionate.

Whilst being full of praise for the bravery and tenacity of the British and Indian troops under his command, he also had a high regard for the conduct of the Japanese in battle, under constant attack from superior forces and lacking adequate supplies.

He told us of an incident in the jungle. Early one morning, he was outside his tent, shaving, using a small mirror attached to a piece of bamboo, when he saw, reflected in the mirror, a movement in the bushes. The next moment two Japanese soldiers appeared, guns pointing in his direction. He swung around, grabbing a sten gun, which he always kept nearby and aimed at the soldiers, killing them both.

"I was just fortunate," he said, "that I happened to point the gun in the right direction." He added that he had had very little practice. The enemy soldiers had infiltrated their lines unknown to them.

He said that we had been doing an important job, safeguarding the integrity of the North West Frontier and were not to feel badly at not being involved in the Burma campaign.

It had been exceptionally hot. Peshawar is surrounded by hills and there is hardly ever any wind. Everybody seemed to be suffering from prickly heat rashes and this included myself. I went to see the medical officer about it and bared my chest to show him the cause of my suffering. He smiled, a little sadly and bared his chest also, to show me that his condition was worse than mine. He told me that there was very little to be done for prickly heat, or *dhobi itch*, as it was also called, since anything applied was soon dissipated by perspiration. The important thing was not to scratch, which was a great temptation, as this caused the rash to spread. He said that I could call in at the treatment room if I wished, but in view of his comments I decided not to bother.

Passing the room where the medical orderly performed his functions, the door opened and David emerged, seemingly in some pain. He was walking like an old man, his knees bent and his legs apart. He told me, as I helped him to his car, that the orderly ('stupid bastard' he called him) had used the wrong substance for his rash – he thought it was liniment – and it had run down his body and onto his genitals, which were also affected by the rash. He was walking with a Cassidy-like stance for several days and not able to accompany his beloved camels on horseback when he was supposed to take them on his last manoeuvre. 'Probably seeking the Holy Grail,' I thought, somewhat disrespectfully.

I suspected that the dhobis who did our washing probably failed to rinse all the soap out of the clothes and to find out if this was true I immersed a newly washed shirt in a bowl of warm water and found that it became soapy. No doubt the presence of dried soap, when dissolved by perspiration, was largely responsible for causing the rashes. I saw the chief *dhobi wallah* and impressed on him the need to have the clothes thoroughly rinsed.

Within a few days only a few of the seats in the mess hall were occupied at meal times. An army lorry pulled up outside the mess one morning while I was having breakfast and I went to see what was being delivered. I had been put in charge of the mess activities.

We were each issued every month with a ration of one bottle of whisky, one bottle of gin and several bottles of Murree beer. The beer was quite good and comparable with the best beer in England, although it was brewed in India. We paid very little for spirits: about ten shillings a bottle for whisky and gin, but these had to be ordered months in advance, as they came from the UK. The lorry was delivering several crates of spirits, mostly for the officers who had since left.

There were about eighty bottles I was unable to dispose of and as it was not prudent to leave them in the mess, I took them back to my bungalow where they lined the shelves in the dining room. We had several parties to celebrate the ending of the war and the bottles slowly disappeared.

I decided to walk to the depot one morning, as I was feeling in need of exercise. I saw the body of a donkey, which had been left by the roadside. When I returned in the evening, only its bones remained. The kite hawks, nature's scavengers, had done their job; one wonders how much more the population of India would suffer from disease if the hawks were not present and the carcasses were just left to putrefy in the heat.

We had another visit from Army headquarters, this time a young brigadier, who was the Director of Supplies and Transport in Delhi. The major was away and so I escorted the brigadier around the depot. He told me that they were becoming short of suitable experienced officers, with the return of many of them to England, and he was looking for a second in command. He asked me if I would be interested in the appointment; he needed someone right away. It would mean immediate promotion to the rank of major and the job would hold out good prospects. I said that I would consider the offer and let him know in a few days time.

The afternoon of the following day, I was called to the main office to take a telephone call from Delhi. They needed my decision immediately as another officer was interested in the job. I had, in fact, already decided not to prolong my stay in India.

I had been thinking of my widowed mother, who had seen very little of me during my nearly seven years in the army. I also considered that the days of the British Raj had run their course and must very soon come to an end. Although the new Indian government would doubtless need the services of some British officers during the period of transition, the chances were that I would soon find myself out of a job and experience difficulty in finding employment back in England after an even more protracted period of absence.

Thus, the day came for me to leave Peshawar. It was a touching experience. When I arrived at the railway station, I found that the whole of the depot personnel, including the major in command and the staff from the petrol depot, some two hundred soldiers, were lining the platform to see me off. I went down the line and shook hands with all of them. Some had tears in their eyes; they are such sentimental people, but I too must confess that I felt very moved.

A subedar major, who I knew very well, said that they saw me as a symbol of the British leaving India and they were very unhappy at the prospect.

For me there had always been a bond, a feeling of mutual respect, a common sense of humour, an inherent kindness on both sides, a tolerance and a brotherhood that transcended colour of skin, religion and social position, However, the occupation of one country by another could not be allowed to continue. I knew that we would be leaving behind something much important than the railways, the irrigation systems, the establishments; a legacy of brotherhood and understanding would not be putting it too strongly.

The Frontier Mail pulled slowly out along the platform, signifying to me the end of my time in the Indian Army. It had been interesting, sometimes exciting, occasionally amusing, but never dull.

I leaned out of the carriage window and waved to the assembled troops. They waved back energetically.

One called out, "Bon voyage, sahib."

Where on earth could he have learnt that?

X: *At Sea with Emily*

I had to wait several days in Deolali, near Bombay, before I was given a passage back to England, killing time around the swimming pool of the small hotel where I had been allotted a room. Bombay was strictly out of bounds to all ranks, I had no idea why, as nobody, I thought, would have been foolish enough to do anything which might jeopardise their return home.

Finally, the day came for my departure and I learned that I would be travelling to Liverpool on the same vessel that had brought me out nearly three years previously, the MV *Georgic*. The voyage would take about two weeks.

It soon became apparent that I was the only Indian Army officer on board, which proved a blessing, as I was not subject to the disciplines which restricted the British Army personnel. I was given a small cabin adjacent to the top deck, where I was to spend a lot of my time, the weather being warm and pleasant. I was able to please myself as to when I got up in the morning and when I took my meals. It was all so different to the outward voyage, when life had verged on the intolerable.

There were several female officers on the ship, I discovered, some army ATS, some navy WRNS and a few QAIMNS nurses. Occasionally I would invite a couple of them to my cabin for tea, but I made sure that I was never left alone with just one of them; it was plain that a few were intent on return-ing to the United Kingdom with a prospective husband in tow and I had no intention of getting myself involved.

On the second evening I stood at the ship's rail, admiring the evening sunset as the ship ploughed its way, almost silently, through the silken waters of the Arabian Sea, with just a faint hiss of the water as it was pushed aside by the bows. In the distance I could hear the subdued thud of the engines, when slowly I became aware of a faint perfume and then the pres-ence of a young Wren officer. She stood close to me, without saying a word and looked at me through the half light. I waited for her to say something but still she remained silent.

"Good evening," I said.

No response. Then, "You are the officer who occupies the cabin near the top deck, are you not?" Her voice was clear and attractive.

"Yes, I am he," I replied.

"Well…" she continued and then paused, as if uncertain how to proceed, "The quarters which have been allotted to us are pretty awful and I was wondering whether I could share your cabin." She let out a sigh of relief at having managed to get the words out. She told me later that it had been an ordeal for her. Before I could even think what to say she went on.

"I would be very discreet. Just sleep there at night, I mean." Another pause. "We are low down in the ship with not much air…" – I recalled my own similar experience when I came out – "and the noise of the engines keeps me awake. Also…" she began to speak rapidly, she clearly wanted to get it all out before I could interrupt, "some of the girls are rather bawdy and not at all nice and I find it rather trying. Mummy and daddy wouldn't like it a bit, me having to put up with their bad language and unladylike behaviour."

I wondered what she had been doing on war service. Some of the types I had been obliged to mix with would have been flattered to have been called just "bawdy".

At last I was able to get a word in.

"But they wouldn't mind you sharing a cabin at night with a man?"

She moved closer.

"But you are an officer and, I am quite sure, a gentleman."

"Maybe," I said, "but even suppose I was, I am still human".

I was beginning to wonder whether she was another of the ladies in search of a husband, but then she seemed too young, not more than 22, and it was apparent that she could easily ensnare a man without resorting to subterfuge. Even in the failing light she was obviously an attractive young lady.

"If I agree to your request, it must be with the understanding that we keep to ourselves. I do not intend to get involved with a woman at the present time. I shall have a great deal to contend with when I get home, after being away for so long."

"Thank you," she said. "I am sure you won't regret it. Will it be alright if I start tonight?"

"Okay, but for goodness sake keep it to yourself. I don't want the chaps to find out. What will you tell your friends?"

"I'll say that I am going to share a cabin at night with a colleague I have just met"

"Well I hope so. Let's make it 9.30. I shall be back from the mess by then. Knock twice. There is a spare bunk with a curtain."

Promptly at 9.30 there was a discreet double knock on the door and I opened it to see her standing there, holding a small suitcase and looking rather coy.

"Do come in," I said. "I wondered whether you would change your mind."

She glided inside and I shut the door.

"Were there any problems?"

"Not really," she said. "I don't think that I am the only one to have found alternative sleeping quarters."

"That doesn't surprise me," I said. "Take off your jacket and come and sit over here for a chat. There is a small wardrobe over there where you can hang your things."

The cabin was quiet comfortably appointed. I understood it to be the pilot's cabin and that I would be required to vacate it when the ship arrived offshore at Liverpool. There were padded seats with backrests and a large table screwed to the floor whereon, no doubt, the pilot put his map to study before taking over the vessel.

She took off her hat and coat, hung them up and sat cross-legged in the corner.

"Very comfortable," she said. "How did you come to get such a nice cabin and all to yourself?"

"You may have noticed," I replied, "that I am Indian Army and all the other military personnel are British Army. I suppose the officer in charge of troops felt that it would be as well if we were segregated. I have no complaints," I added.

"1 should think not," she said. A pause. "Would you like a drink? I have only Vat 69 and Gordon's. I drink scotch but I know the navy prefers gin"

"Not for me," she replied." Actually, I never drink alcohol. Daddy warned me that I could get into trouble, especially in a hot climate, if I got into the habit of drinking. "Easy to get carried away," he said.

"1 quite understand," I replied. "You couldn't have found it easy when all your companions were drinking. How about a coffee? I have one of those coffee-making machines I found out I could plug in. I carry it with me on my travels. Comes in very useful."

"That would be very nice," she replied." I haven't any milk though," I said.

"Never mind, I quite like black coffee if it is hot. My name's Emily, by the way."

"I'm Bill," I replied.

Sipping the coffee, I asked her where she had been before she came to join the ship in Bombay.

"I was stationed in Calcutta, attached to Naval Intelligence," she said.

"I was at a supply depot in Peshawar, on the North West Frontier," I responded. "I visited Calcutta only a few months ago, on leave with a friend. We didn't stay long. The dhobis were on strike, as were the sweepers. We couldn't get any clothes cleaned and there were piles of stinking rubbish everywhere. We were glad to get away." I told her of our experience with the mobs.

"We stayed at the Grand Hotel in Chowringhee," I continued.

"I know the hotel," said Emily. "I called there a couple of times to see my friend Daphne. She was staying there with her mother. They had been seeing off her father, Brigadier Ferguson, who had been given a clearing-up job in Burma."

"What a coincidence!" I exclaimed. "The brigadier was the commanding officer in Peshawar. I too saw Daphne at the hotel. It was a chance meeting. I had seen her a few times in Peshawar."

"I don't believe it! You knew Daphne?"

"Yes, but not very well," I lied. "Just a passing acquaintance. How strange you should know her."

"Know her!" Emily exclaimed. "We were at school together. She was always getting herself into trouble with the local lads. Despite what you say, I couldn't see her letting you off Scot free. I bet you could tell me a few things of interest."

"I am going to turn in soon," I said. "Would you like to use the wardroom first, or shall I?"

"You go first," she replied. "I always take a long time."

"Incidentally," I said. "I always take a shower as soon as I get up."

"So do I," she responded, then seeing my face added with a mischievous laugh, "don't worry, I wasn't going to suggest that we took one together!"

I laughed too. I couldn't help feeling attracted to her.

'What have I let myself in for,' I wondered.

"Well Emily," I said, "I wish you goodnight. Sleep well. I'll give you a call in the morning when I have finished in the wardroom and then I'll make my way down to the mess and leave the cabin to you. Do make sure that you close the door properly when you leave. See you again in the evening. I'll make sure that I'm back by nine-thirty.

During the day I wandered around the ship, hoping, I must confess, that I would come across Emily, but the vessel was very crowded. She was probably with her friends down below.

When the evening came and after I had finished dinner, I was asked by one of the chaps to join him in a game of chess, but I declined, as it could go on for hours and I couldn't leave Emily waiting outside the cabin door. I was beginning to think I had been foolish to agree to her request, but then I had to concede that I was enjoying the prospect of her company in the evenings.

We still had a week to go before we reached England. The truth was that I could not get Hilda out of my mind, fool though I was not to acknowledge that it was all over between us. I suppose that in a way. I was still in love with her – or with the memories of her.

Emily was late arriving. I had begun to wonder whether she had had second thoughts about sleeping in the cabin, although I had treated her with every consideration. It was nearly ten o'clock when she finally knocked on the door. I had taken a few drinks with the chaps, to celebrate our return home, more whisky than I was used to and had fallen asleep. She must have knocked several times before I was awoken and I staggered to the door to let her in. She started to apologise for being late, but I interrupted her to say it didn't matter.

Just at that moment the ship gave a lurch and I staggered backwards towards the corner seat, the momentum carrying Emily with me. We ended up together, sprawling on the seat, Emily in a most unladylike, position. It was clear that her friends had persuaded her to take a drink or two and not being used to alcohol, it was having a devastating effect on her. The next moment she had her arms around my neck and was fast asleep. I wondered what mummy and daddy would have thought if they could have seen her.

I was able to get to my feet with Emily in my arms, laid her on her bunk, took off her jacket – she hadn't been wearing a hat, probably lost it – and her shoes and covered her with a light blanket. It was quite warm in the cabin, even with the portholes open. I went to have a wash and to clean my teeth, changed and got into bed. I left a subdued light on in case Emily wanted to get up during the night.

Morning came. It was just after seven o'clock and Emily was still asleep. I decided not to disturb her but to go for an early breakfast so that she would have the cabin to herself. I tried not to make any noise while I was in the wardroom, having a shower, but I must have disturbed her as she called out.

"I shan't be long… Just having a shower!" I yelled. I hurried to finish and dry myself down and quickly donned a shirt and some slacks I kept handy. I didn't have a dressing gown.

Emily was sitting on the bunk, looking rather the worse for her previous night's experience.

"Whatever happened?" she asked.

"Well…" I said, "you had obviously been drinking and you were in no state for conversation when you arrived last night."

"Was I awful?" she asked.

"Not in the least." I assured her. "You just staggered into the room and ended up sitting on my lap with your arms around my neck".

"You must think I was terrible," she said.

"Of course not," I replied. "I gathered that your chums had managed to persuade you to take some drinks and you had been somewhat overcome."

"Did you mind?" she asked. "I mean, me acting in a familiar way?"

"Not a bit," I replied. "I rather enjoyed it."

"And then you put me to bed?"

157

"Well I only took your jacket and shoes off. You seem to have lost your hat."

"You could have taken advantage of me," she said. "Why didn't you?"

"My goodness," I said, you don't really think I would have tried to make love to you in your condition?"

"Some chaps would have," she said. "You really are a gentleman."

I decided to end the conversation.

"I'm just off to breakfast. I don't suppose you will be going?"

"No," she replied. "I couldn't face it. So this is what it is like, getting drunk. I feel pretty rotten."

"It will soon pass," I said, "but you must have something to eat. You stay here and I'll bring you something back."

I didn't stay long over breakfast, but long enough, I considered, for Emily to tidy herself up. I brought her back a couple of bread rolls, some pats of butter and some jam in a small pot.

"Would you like me to make you a coffee?" I asked.

"Yes please, I think it will help me to shake off this hangover. It's the first time I have experienced it. I think I'll be sure to stay off the booze in future."

"You can stay here as long as you like," I said. I'm going for a stroll along the deck and I may see if any of the chaps would like a game of chess. If you are gone when I get back, I'll see you again this evening... Sober, I hope," I added with a smile.

"You need have no fear of that," Emily replied. "Thank you so much for being so kind to me."

"It has been a pleasure," I said, as I made for the door.

As the few remaining days passed, I began to look forward more and more to the evenings, when Emily would arrive. She always seemed pleased to see me and we enjoyed each other's company for the brief period before we made for our bunks. I found myself lying awake, thinking what a lovely girl she was, but knowing that we were not likely to meet again after we went our separate ways on arrival at Liverpool. I thought also of Daphne, wondering when she would be returning to England with her mother. I still had here telephone number somewhere. There would be no harm in giving her a ring. She might even agree to meet me again.

Then thoughts of Hilda entered my mind; what a different homecoming it would have been if only she had waited for me. But what had I to offer any girl? Apart from the little, money I had managed to save – I had been sending my mother a substantial amount each month – there was just my army gratuity to keep me going until I found a job. Both Daphne and Emily obviously belonged to well off families. I had mixed feelings about the future.

One morning I got up early and wandered into the wardroom for a shower, only to find that Emily had decided to take an early shower also. She was not in the least put out at me seeing her without any clothes on.

"Shan't be long," was all she said, as I beat a hasty retreat. She shortly appeared with a towel wrapped around her.

"Sorry about that," I said.

"My fault," she responded. "I usually wait for you to finish, but you were asleep when I woke and I thought I would get a shower in before you surfaced. I hope you were not shocked at seeing me naked."

"Shocked?" I repeated. "No. It was a delightful experience."

"Like to see me again?" she said, letting the towel fall to the floor.

She came towards me, her arms outstretched. How could I refuse her?

The two nights remaining we spent in each others arms, lying on blankets on the floor. After all, as she said, they were doing it all over the ship. I wondered dreamily, how she could know?

XI: *Home and Hilda*

We both awoke very early on the last morning and I suggested to Emily that we went on deck to see if we could sight land. We took blankets with us as protection against the cold morning air. It seemed bitterly cold after the heat we had become accustomed to in India.

No one else was about, except for a couple of chaps sweeping the deck. In the distance could be seen some lights twinkling minutely on the horizon. From a map I had studied in the ship's lounge, I took them to be those of Milford Haven in Wales. We were nearly home.

Emily turned to me and said, "I suppose I shan't be seeing you again once we leave the ship?"

"I'd love to see you again, of course…" I replied, "but I am going to be very busy after such a long time away. My mother isn't very well and I feel that I should devote all my attention to her. I live in Kent, by the way. Where is your home?"

"In Buckingham," she replied. "I'll give you our phone number and when you feel free to come up to town you can give me a ring and I'll try to meet you. I have so much enjoyed the last few days, or rather evenings … not forgetting the nights," she added with a mischievous smile.

"Me too," I said. "It has been an unforgettable experience. A most delightful finale to my war service."

There was silence between us, then she turned to me again. This time I could see by the early morning light that her eyes were glistening with tears.

"Tell me that you love me and will never leave me," she said.

I was taken aback. I didn't know what to say.

"I can't bear the thought of not seeing you again," she continued.

"Dear Emily," I said, "I think you're a lovely girl and it has been marvellous knowing you, but you must be sensible. We don't really know each other and we may have little in common. When you get home with your family, our short affair will soon become a memory. You must have several male acquaintances coming back from the war who will be delighted to see you."

"It is true," she replied, still tearful. "I do have a number of men friends, but you are the first man I have really felt close to. I suppose you are right..." she paused, "you will try to see me again, won't you?"

"I promise to contact you again as soon as I get settled," I replied. "Give me your phone number when we get back to the cabin."

We both returned to the cabin after breakfast to say our farewell. I had to admit to myself that I was sorry to have to say goodbye to Emily. I had become very fond of her. I assured her again that I would be in touch before long and we both left for our disembarkation assembly points, the vessel having docked while we were having breakfast.

I had gone in search of the officer in charge and when I had eventually found him he was, of course, frantically busy and more or less brushed me aside, telling me that he was not concerned with Indian Army personnel and I would have to make my own way home and contact the India Office on my arrival.

Trains were waiting to take the troops to the demobilisation centres. I watched as they poured down the gangways with their kitbags and luggage. I felt somehow detached from the proceedings. I suppose in reality I *was* detached; they were of a different army.

Anxious as I was to get home, I did not fancy scrambling down the gangway among a sea of men. I decided to wait until they had all disembarked, hoping that I would be able to get some assistance with my luggage, which consisted of a heavy leather suitcase I had bought when I visited Agra with Max, and a heavy steel trunk.

The men were being assembled in ranks on the quayside. The familiar tones of the NCOs rang out loud and clear. I knew that this would be my final contact with the military. I was almost a civilian again. Just awaiting my discharge papers, left to resume the life that had been interrupted so suddenly such a long time ago.

There was no one to help me with the luggage and I had to make two trips up and down the gangway. I had collected quite a number of articles on my travels, most of which were contained in the trunk, and it was exceedingly heavy.

Eventually I made it to the platform for the London trains and the train for Liverpool Street Station was not long in coming. I was grateful to have the assistance of a porter. He was an elderly man, but surprisingly strong and I was impressed with his courtesy. He had probably lived through the bombing of Liverpool, clearly too old for military service. Sadly, I had no English money and was not able to give him a tip.

The luggage was loaded into a van and I took my seat in an empty compartment with a sigh of relief. Very few people were going up to London.

Arriving in London, I obtained a trolley on which to load my luggage and I made for the office of the Railway Transport Officer. He was able to advance me some money.

I had been given a travel warrant by the troopship officer, which covered me for my journey home, but I still needed money for a taxis and for a meal at the station. Frugal, still rationed food, but it was nice to be back again and the meal wasn't all that bad.

Taxis were difficult to come by and I had to wait a considerable time for one outside the station. Eventually one turned up and I assisted the driver in carrying the trunk from the trolley.

"What have you got in here mate?" he asked. "You been robbing one of those temples?"

We skirted the City on the way to Victoria Station and I was appalled at the devastation. Much effort had clearly been made in removing the rubble, but it was going to take many years to bring London back to its former glory. St Paul's Cathedral had been spared and stood miraculously isolated among scores of demolished buildings.

When we arrived at Victoria Station, I was lucky in finding two military policemen on duty outside, who very obligingly lugged the trunk and the case to the platform and then onto the train which, by good fortune, was about to depart for my home station. The train took just over an hour to arrive.

The porter phoned for the local taxi and I was soon on the final leg of my journey home.

I arrived to find that my mother was out, which was a great disappointment, but of course she could not have known when I would arrive back. I knocked at the house next door and the neighbours were kind enough to invite me in for a cup of tea. I sat by the window so that I could see when my mother returned and it was not long before she arrived.

I excused myself and thanked the neighbours for their kindness, promising to call again to tell them of some of my experiences in India. They had lost two sons in the war.

I arrived just as my mother was closing the door. She didn't look very well. It had been a hard time for her, one way and another. After our greetings I managed to manoeuvre the luggage inside and we sat and chatted. It was a strange experience for me. I have often heard people say that when they arrived back after a long spell it was as if they had never been away. This was not so for me, but then, this was not the house I had left to join the army. It had been demolished in an air raid soon after… and I would never see my brother again.

My mother said that sometimes at night she still imagined she could hear the awful droning noise of German bombers overhead.

She told me that a letter had arrived for me some time earlier and I saw from the postmark and the writing, that it was from Hilda. My mother disappeared discreetly into the kitchen to allow me to read the letter in private. She had no doubt deduced who the sender was.

My hands trembled as I tore open the envelope and removed the contents. I can recall every word of the letter.

"Dear Bill," it began, "I am writing to you at your home as I should think that now the war is over with Japan, you must be coming back soon, although you may not want to open the letter as you will know that it is from me.

"When I wrote to you in Peshawar, I didn't tell you much about what had happened and I would like you to know and, I hope, understand. Soon after you left for India I had to give up teaching the piano as there were so few pupils and I was obliged to start work in the assembly rooms of the aircraft factory near Cowes. I was very miserable, not knowing when, or if, I would be seeing you again.

"1 did want so much to visit you in London before you were sent abroad, but my parents persuaded me not to as they were worried about the bombing. They always tried to dominate me, being their only child, I suppose. It was through their

166

influence that I became engaged. I never did care very much for David. As you know, I called off the engagement, rather late in the day, I'm afraid. It was mean of me, not telling you of the engagement until later. I didn't want to lose you.

"I sometimes went to the restaurant in Gurnard, where we used to meet and I occasionally played the piano. But then I stopped going, as I kept thinking of the lovely times we spent together and this made me sad.

"One evening after work, the shop floor foreman asked me to go with him for a drink and as I was feeling rather low I agreed. As you know, I never drank much alcohol and the few drinks I had made me very drunk and not able to resist his advances. When I discovered that I was pregnant I was horrified. I stopped writing to you and your letters became more and more distraught. You must have been very worried

"At last I found the courage to write. You seemed at first to be prepared to forgive me and I hoped that we might still be able to carry on as before, but then your letters became bitter and I knew that it was over between us. Of course I understand how you must have felt, so far away, feeling betrayed. It is very hard to suffer as I have for making one foolish mistake. I still love you deeply and always will. I don't suppose you care much for me now. David offered to marry me when he heard that I was pregnant.

"He is a nice man, although my feelings towards him are not very warm, but I suppose I am happy in a way. I have always loved children and Susan is a lovely baby. I wish she were yours.

"Do you think that you could come over to the Island to see me? I can't bear the thought of never seeing you again. I could get a friend to mind Susan and I could meet you off the ferry at Ryde. Please, please write to say you will come. I promise not to make a fool of myself. You can use my maiden name when you write and send the letter to my parents address, above. I have told them everything and they are very sad for both of us. I will wait for your letter, praying that it will tell me you are coming.

You must, please!

Pip. (That was her nickname that everybody used.)

I sat for quite some time, my mind in a whirl. Then I read the letter again. She was quite right, I had felt bitter and badly let down. Now, I had to confess, time had mellowed my thoughts and I was half wishing that I had asked her to marry me, despite the baby… but of course it was too late.

I sent her a brief letter. I wrote that I would love to see her again and despite everything she had always been in my thoughts. 'I can come over to the Island whenever it suits you. I'll find out the times of the trains from Waterloo and the times of the connecting ferries from Portsmouth. Just give me a date and I'll catch the first train.'

Two days later her letter arrived, in reply to mine. She was overjoyed that I was going to see her. She said that the following Wednesday would be an easy day for, her to have the baby minded.

I wrote back at once to tell her that I would be on the eleven a.m. ferry to Ryde on Wednesday, arriving there at about midday.

I had not kept my mother fully informed, but now I decided to tell her the whole story. She was very sympathetic about the way things had turned out, but she did not think it foolish of me to see Hilda again.

"It is the only way you will be able to put your mind at rest," she said.

The journey to the Island was uneventful. I had decided to travel in my uniform. For one thing, most of my clothes had gone up in flames when our house was bombed, also, Hilda had only ever seen me in uniform and it somehow seemed to be more appropriate that I should meet her again dressed in khaki. Another reason was, that as an officer I would be travelling first class on the train from Waterloo and would probably have a compartment to myself in which to collect my thoughts. This proved to be the case.

The ferry was more or less on time and as soon as it docked I spotted Hilda on the quayside. There was no mistaking her. I do believe that she was wearing the same dress as the one she wore when I last saw her nearly three years earlier, but then she would not have been able to buy new clothes because of wartime restrictions.

She saw me and began to wave frantically. I waved back. As I walked down the gangway of the ferry my knees turned to jelly. I wondered what I was going to say to her in welcome. As soon as my feet were on the jetty, she came running to me

169

and threw herself into my arms. This was typical Hilda behaviour. Her emotions always governed her behaviour.

I was compelled to hold her tightly. Tears began to well up in my eyes as the realisation came to me that she was no longer mine. I had lost her. She must have understood how I was feeling. She stepped back to look at me.

"I am so very, very sorry," she said. There were tears in her eyes too.

We walked to the end of the jetty, holding each other around the waist, not saying a word. In fact I hadn't spoken at all, there was too big a lump in my throat. That same perfume she had always worn tugged at my heart.

We made for a restaurant we had sometimes visited when I was stationed in Ryde, not far from the pier, just across the road. We ordered a snack and then sat at a small table near the window, just looking at each other. She placed a hand on the table and I covered it with one of mine. She bowed her head and tears ran down her face.

"Don't cry," I said, trying not to do so myself, "All is forgiven."

"You are making it difficult for me," she said tearfully. "I would find it easier if you were upset and told me how badly I have behaved and ruined everything for us."

"But I have had a long time to think about it," I said, "and I have come to accept that you have now made a life without me, however painful it is for both of us."

We ate our meal in silence. Hilda asked me when I would be going back and I told her I intended to stay the night at a hotel in Newport after looking around my old haunts. I would be getting the ferry back to Portsmouth late in the afternoon. I would have liked to have stayed longer had it not been for my mother.

Hilda asked me whether she could see me again the next day, as she felt sure that her mother would mind the baby for her.

"Of course I'll see you again," I said. I wanted to make it as easy as I could for her, although I knew that I was being rather cowardly in wanting to put off our final farewell for as long as possible. "Why not bring the baby along," I said. "I would love to see her"

"Would you really?" she said, brightening up. "As a matter of fact, our house is quite near Gurnard and I often walk the pram along the promenade. This was where we had spent so much of our time together and I wondered' whether it would be a good idea. However, I agreed to meet her near the restaurant at midday. I did not know whether she had told her husband that I had come to see her, but I decided not to ask. She had mentioned that he worked now on the other side of the Island.

The next morning, after breakfast at the hotel, I caught the bus which went first to Cowes and then, after a ten minute wait, on to Gurnard. I arrived there about eleven and as it was a nice day, now late summer, I decided to go for a walk to kill time along the promenade. I met a chap we used to know, who looked after the beach huts. He recognised me and told me that he had heard what had happened and made some derogatory remarks about Hilda. I made it clear that I didn't want to discuss the matter. I was trying not to feel sad and sentimental, but I found it difficult. It was probably a great mistake to have come back, but it was late in the day to do anything about it now.

Just after twelve Hilda arrived with the pram. It was a lovely baby. She smiled at me and I asked Hilda if I could push the pram. This seemed both to surprise and to delight her.

So there I was, resplendent in my Indian Army uniform, pushing a pram along the promenade, containing a baby belonging to a girl, married to another man, who had promised undying love to me! How strange and stupid of me!

We went into the restaurant for an early tea and Hilda played the piano for us. Susan seemed to enjoy the music.

The time came for me to leave, to catch the bus back to Newport. This time Hilda pushed the pram, towards the end of the promenade, from where a steep hill arose, at the top of which was the bus stop. We came to a halt and turned to face each other. We held each other tightly, for the last time and we kissed passionately. She turned the pram and proceeded along the promenade, towards the cafes, not looking back. Tears ran down my face. 'You bloody fool,' I said to myself, not really knowing why.

The bus was late in arriving at Newport and I missed the one that would have taken me to Ryde in time for the ferry I had planned to sail on. This would have connected with the train from Portsmouth to Waterloo. When the next bus finally arrived for Ryde, the driver, when he alighted, turned out to be a chap I had known when I was stationed at Wilton House.

He was, in fact, the despatch rider who had brought the teleprinter message about the approach of the enemy barges towards the Island. We recognised each other immediately and after a chat I mentioned that I had missed the earlier bus to connect with the ferry.

"Don't worry about that," he said. "I'll see you get there on time." And he kept his word. He drove like the wind, to the consternation of most of the passengers; he ignored the people waiting at the request stops and stopped only for brief moments to let people off.

He got me there on time, although I had to run along the pier and only just made it onto the ferry.

When I arrived back home, I found a letter awaiting me from the India Office in London, thanking me for my services and informing me that I had been granted the honorary rank of captain. More important, a cheque was enclosed for my back pay and my gratuity. I took my mother out for a sumptuous lunch.

Now for the future, back in the real world, knowing nothing of the interesting and exciting experiences that lay ahead of me...

End